ECONOMIST
GANDHI

ECONOMIST GANDHI

THE ROOTS AND THE RELEVANCE OF THE POLITICAL ECONOMY OF THE MAHATMA

JAITHIRTH RAO

FOREWORD BY
RAJMOHAN GANDHI

PORTFOLIO
PENGUIN

An imprint of Penguin Random House

PORTFOLIO

USA | Canada | UK | Ireland | Australia
New Zealand | India | South Africa | China

Portfolio is part of the Penguin Random House group of companies
whose addresses can be found at global.penguinrandomhouse.com

Published by Penguin Random House India Pvt. Ltd
4th Floor, Capital Tower 1, MG Road,
Gurugram 122 002, Haryana, India

Penguin
Random House
India

First published in Portfolio by Penguin Random House India 2021

10 9 8 7 6 5 4 3 2 1

ISBN 9780670096237

Typeset in Adobe Garamond Pro by Manipal Technologies Limited, Manipal
Printed at Replika Press Pvt. Ltd, India

www.penguin.co.in

Contents

Foreword

Approaching Gandhi from uncustomary places, Jaithirth Rao makes original and provocative points in this enjoyable book. While its title might surprise those unaware of Gandhi's involvement with economics, the book also enlightens the reader with some of Gandhi's views on ethics, religion, human nature and society.

The writer is a businessman and entrepreneur convinced about Burkean conservatism. Something alerts me that he and I are unlikely to take identical views on India's politics. But I respect (and envy) Rao's apparent ease in multiple worlds: business economics, European cultural history, Sanskrit and more.

And including, now, Gandhian thought. The author seems to have captured aspects of Gandhi's thinking usually missed by those who are sure they know their Gandhi.

If the thinker Gandhi is portrayed in these pages, the observer-empiricist Gandhi, too, will be found. Also noticed by Rao is a usually undetected facet of Gandhi's: his feminine-maternal side.

Confronting Gandhi the economist, the author identifies a key Gandhi focus—the consumer. Concerned as Gandhi is with the worker in a plant, with the mill's owner, and with the spinner and weaver of khadi, he is just as keen, Rao shows, on the consumer of the cloth, or of anything else jointly created by labour and capital.

The author also gives us his understanding of Gandhi's conception of an ascetic, dedicated or soul-filled life. Rao's Gandhi insists that a spiritual life has to involve service to fellow humans. To renounce this world and yet serve its residents was Gandhi's prescription for himself and others.

Rao also shows that the Gandhi, who drastically reduced his personal wants, never elevated poverty. It was rather the opposite. Wounded by India's poverty, Gandhi wanted everyone to enjoy a decent level of life.

The Gandhi unveiled by Rao is brilliant, unexpected and daring. Also, almost always this is a smiling Gandhi. He is very human, too. In his humanity, Rao's Gandhi is equal to everyone else, including the writer, who himself seems to smile while writing about Gandhi.

One of the most charming things about Gandhi is that he allows writers—encourages them, makes it easy for them—to write freely about him. If only other famous figures had this quality!

Rao reveals the impish Gandhi. Absent from these pages, however, is the anguished Gandhi, the one acquainted with grief. This is not a complaint. Why should every portrait be complete?

Rao's familiarity with European cultural history enables him to recognize the influence on Gandhi of Western thinking. Just as the wants-reducing Gandhi was also a foe of poverty, the passionately Indian Gandhi also kept his mind's windows and doors open, letting in light from all sides.

Rao's discussion of Gandhi's Nai Talim—or New Education—and of trusteeship seems to offer fresh insights. The tinkerer/experimenter Gandhi identified by Rao in his analysis of Nai Talim is unknown to most. Rao's discovery of this Gandhi is bound to intrigue readers.

His reflections on Gandhi's fascination for the Isa Upanishad, and on Gandhi's use of that Upanishad as a foundation for his theory of trusteeship, also convey an original flavour.

Gandhi did not compose the lines of 'Ishwar Allah Tere Naam', or of 'Vaishnava Jana To', or of the Isa Upanishad. He merely repeated them. But Gandhi's soul was in those lines, and those lines were in his soul. He and the lines are in eternal union.

I congratulate Jaithirth Rao on this refreshing study and commend it to the reader.

Urbana, Illinois, USA   Rajmohan Gandhi

1

Introduction

Gandhi, a Man of Many Facets

The Italian scholar Ugo Caruso has this to say about a chapter he contributed to a book on Gandhi's thoughts: 'The sheer volume of the material written by and on Gandhi has forced me to embark on a process of selection . . . I have tried to maintain, as far as possible, an equitable and impartial position in the midst of the many perspectives from which the figure of Gandhi can be analysed' (Pföstl, 2013). I have attempted in this book to do pretty much the opposite. I have tried to maintain as partial a position as possible and selectively quote from writings by Gandhi and about Gandhi to argue that we can and should look at the Mahatma as being an original and seminal thinker in the intellectual discourse around market capitalism. As it turned out, I received enthusiastic support for this approach from the philosopher Akeel Bilgrami (who certainly qualifies to be a member of the Marxist school) when he spoke to me about it, albeit with a twinkle in his eye. Professor Bilgrami has of course made connections between the so-called spiritual Gandhi and the so-called materialist Marx (Pföstl, 2013). Gandhi's contribution in the area of what is best described as applied economics, with particular relevance to the managerial agency problem articulated early in the history of economic thought by the 'father' of economics, Adam Smith himself (Smith, 1982), by way of the doctrine of 'trusteeship' (CW, 1999, v. 43, p. 497; v. 70, p. 423), is clearly one that has resounding relevance as we grapple with the problems of corporate governance in contemporary times. It is striking to note that none of the academic writers on this subject has referred to the Mahatma. This book attempts to firmly place Gandhi's ethical thought—at least in so far as it relates to business, wealth, the management of businesses, the management of wealth, and the management of inheritance—in a tradition of economic philosophy that is long and possibly hoary. By linking Gandhi's thoughts with the insights on identity economics provided by the Nobel laureate George Akerlof and his colleague Rachel Kranton (Akerlof and Kranton, 2010), I believe it is possible to develop a theoretically sound and eminently practical approach to contemporary problems in corporate governance. There is no single silver bullet for dealing with what many consider to be a crisis in modern capitalism, business practices and the management of wealth. When Gandhi died, very few persons would have predicted that Martin Luther King, Lech Walesa and Nelson Mandela would all end up leading significant movements, in some measure as Gandhi's disciples. Despite the temptation for us Indians to claim Gandhi as our own, there is something universal about Gandhi's contributions. Ramachandra Guha has drawn our attention to this (Guha, 2013). Gandhi is on record as having said that 'modern civilization would be a good idea'. The Gandhian scholar Rajni Bakshi points out that Gandhi never castigated 'Western' civilization; he merely poked fun at 'modern' civilization (Bakshi, 2012). Given that market capitalism is so ubiquitously associated with modern civilization, is it fair to fall back on Gandhi? Gandhi was a practitioner and a votary of asceticism. And did he not go on record to say that he was a socialist? (CW, 1999, v. 29, p. 266). Bilgrami even makes the case that Gandhi had an inherently anti-capitalist bias; capitalism was one of the features of modern civilization that Gandhi was opposed to (Bilgrami, 2014).

While all of this certainly casts doubt on our stated purpose of making Gandhi an unlikely guru for students of the economics of market capitalism, it must be pointed out that Gandhi was a personality quite comfortable living with massive contradictions, articulating at different points in time widely divergent opinions. Hence a strong case can be made that Gandhi can not only be used to bolster ascetic anti-consumerist movements, but also be used by those who make their living exploring the challenges of contemporary market-based systems.

Gandhi had proposed a radical system and methodology for school education through the Nai Talim or New Learning programme. This approach places 'tinkering' at the heart of learning and skill development. It deserves to be studied and explored as the Mahatma's unique contribution in the area of the economics of human capital development. What cannot be denied is that almost invariably, Gandhi has something original, even seminal, to contribute to modern thought. To underestimate the significance and sheer depth of the views of the man would be a grievous mistake.

Gandhi Was Not Anti-Business or Anti-Capitalist

Rajni Bakshi writes: 'Gandhi's asceticism in later life tends to obscure the fact that he often reminded people that he is a "*vanika putra*", the son of a baniya (merchant)' (Bakshi, 2012). In another context, Gandhi's American admirer William Shirer writes: 'There was something of the banian trader in Gandhi, reflecting the caste from which he came'(Shirer, 1980); and Gandhi himself remained a supporter of the caste system, although he did hedge himself even as early as in 1921, when he wrote in *Young India* as follows: 'I believe in the varnashrama dharma in a sense, in my opinion, strictly Vedic but not in its present popular and crude sense' (CW, 1999, v. 24, p. 371). Gandhi's attempt at a nuanced distinction between the caste system and the so-called traditional *varnashrama dharma* remained with him all his life. Gandhi's positive approach to business, trade and wealth may have been in part a function of his caste origins. It was also reflected in many of his actions. He went to South Africa as an attorney for Gujarati Muslin merchants who themselves originally belonged to the Bania caste and were relatively recent converts to Islam. In South Africa, two of his important associates, Polack and Kallenbach, were Jewish businessmen (Guha, 2013). Back in India, Gandhi was quite close to Ambalal Sarabhai, who provided funds for Gandhi's ashram in Ahmedabad. Gandhi was also close to the Marwari Bania businessman Jamnalal Bajaj, who was sometimes referred to as Gandhi's fifth son. Gandhi maintained very close contacts with businessmen like Ghanshyamdas Birla. In fact, what is today called the Tees January Marg in Delhi was the site of Birla House. It was here that Nathu Ram Godse shot the Mahatma. Gandhi was Birla's guest on that fateful thirtieth day of January in 1948 (Guha, 2018). Gandhi took positive delight in the business successes of India and Indians. He was ecstatic when the Scindia Steam Navigation Company launched a ship under an Indian flag (CW, 1999, v. 39, p. 335). The evolution of the caste system, trade and finance networks, and organized charity in Gandhi's home state of Gujarat, clearly influenced Gandhi in the development of his own admittedly idiosyncratic, but equally insightful and powerful views in the field of political economy. The historian Chhaya Goswami points out that in Kachchh, the king always appointed a merchant, usually of a Bania caste like the Bhatias, as his diwan or prime minster. It could also quite easily be a merchant from a traditionally peasant or artisan caste (Goswami, 2016). This contrasts with what obtained in other parts of India, where the ministers were usually Brahmins. The rulers of the different states of Gujarat saw the merchant elite as their allies. They respected the office of the Nagarsheth, who was the leader of the merchant community across caste and religious divides. Interestingly, according to Goswami, the Nagarsheth acted as a trustee of the interests of his fraternity. The Panjrapoles, the animal hospitals that were dear to the hearts of the vegetarian Jain and Vaishnava Banias of Gujarat, were run as charitable trusts (Goswami, 2016).

The famous Anandji Kalyanji Trust, which manages several Jain temples across India, is said to have been established between 1630 and 1640, although accurate recording goes back only till 1720. The chief trustee of the Anandji Kalyanji Trust for over fifty years, Kasturbhai Lalbhai, was a lifelong friend and associate of Gandhi (Desai, 1983). One can make the case that the Bania-trustee tradition of Gujarat was very much part of Gandhi's own Bania-Vaishnava world view, and over the years helped him refine his ideas of trusteeship. This argument is made in depth in Chapter 3.

Lawyer Gandhi

It is important to remember that Gandhi was a lawyer trained in English common law traditions. It stands to reason that, along with his acquaintanceship with the Magna Carta, the great charter guaranteeing political liberties to English citizens, which had the unintended consequence of making him a lifelong seditionist, he picked up, among other things, a sound understanding of the legal concept of trusteeship at the Inner Temple, one of the four Inns of Court in London. A peculiarity that is central to trusteeship is that the trustee does not act in his or her own interest, but in the interests of another legal person who is known as the beneficiary. This is a foundational idea, which Gandhi developed further in ways that were both brilliant and idiosyncratic, pretty much what one would expect from the Mahatma! Trusteeship is a concept fairly unique to English common law. It does not exist in continental civil law and Code Napoleon jurisdictions (Macfarlane, 2002). During an illuminating conversation, Girish Dave, himself a feisty Gujarati lawyer with an impish Gandhian sense of rebellion about him, told me that had Gandhi trained in France, which is a civil-law country, he might have been less committed both to non-violent Constitutional progress and to trusteeship. Trusteeship is considered one of the high points of English common law and almost as a unique contribution in the broader area of civil and commercial jurisprudence (Scott, 1922).

Closely associated with the idea of trusteeship is the idea of what constitutes 'fiduciary responsibility' and abuse thereof. The fiduciary notion assumes that the trustee is not selfishly pursuing the trustee's own interests, but is keeping in mind the interests of the beneficiary. The trustee acts on behalf of 'another person' and is duty-bound to protect and enhance the interests of the 'other'. The moralist in Gandhi clearly saw the relationship between this legal concept and the ethical imperative for unselfishness. A violation of one's fiduciary responsibilities as a trustee is contrary to law and can invite legal sanctions and penalties. It was Gandhi's genius not to just stay focused on the illegality, but also highlight the immorality of neglect of fiduciary duties. Gandhi pointed out that Hindu tradition stresses not only 'paapa' (sin); the act of being a good trustee could also lead to 'punya' (meritorious action, or the opposite of sin). Gandhi was very fond of and extremely influenced by the Gospels of the New Testament. Arguably, he quotes more from the Gospels than from any other source. Among the Christian denominations, the Quakers caught his attention, and Gandhi developed a keen interest in their philosophy. The Quakers were a group of anti-establishment Christians who were pioneers in a variety of fields: opposition to slavery, support for Irish and Indian nationalism and support of principled pacifism. As an aside, it is interesting that Gandhi's first public speech during his Round Table Conference visit to England was in front of Quakers at the Friends Meeting House in Euston Road in London (Guha, 2011). The Quakers were a Christian denomination whose commitment to absolutist standards of non-violence is well known. What is not so well known is that Quakers had ideological concerns in the area of inheritance, including inheritance of wealth. While several Quakers opposed the idea of humans being born into bondage as slaves, others have repeatedly looked upon inherited wealth as being problematic (Gulley, 2013). Gandhi too was extremely uncomfortable with inherited wealth. He was quite emphatic in the *Harijan* in 1942 when he wrote: 'Personally I do not believe in inherited riches.' (CW, 1999, v. 82, p. 63).

Gandhi and Western Intellectual Traditions

The classic book *Hind Swaraj* has an overwhelming position among Gandhi's writings. Till the end, Gandhi maintained that the book reflected his positions accurately. In *Hind Swaraj*, Gandhi attacked the endless pursuit of material wants, so characteristic of modern civilization as Gandhi saw it (Parel, HS, 2009). In *Hind Swaraj*, Gandhi interrogated the very idea of 'progress' in the context of the aftermath of the Industrial Revolution (Parel, HS, 2009). This, and his focus on human 'needs' as distinct from human 'wants', would suggest that Gandhi had a built-in bias against modern capitalism. Gandhi, in his words and his actions, tried to minimize his consumption levels. This goes against the popular conception of capitalism being based on ever-increasing consumption. Bilgrami makes this point when he asserts that Gandhi was in the camp opposite to that of the Scottish Enlightenment philosophers, Adam Smith and David Hume, who are in many respects the foundational thinkers associated with market capitalism; and Bilgrami would extend this further to establish a connection with Marx on the basis of Gandhi's inherent anti-capitalism (Bilgrami, 2012). The masterly American scholars of Indian history, Lloyd and Susanne Rudolph, see a connection between Gandhi and the 'other' West inhabited by the English critic John Ruskin, the American philosopher Thoreau and the Russian novelist Leo Tolstoy (Rudolph and Rudolph, 2010). We have already noted Gandhi's associations with the 'other' Christians—the Quakers. To think of Gandhi as a political economist who has contributed to the intellectual development of modern capitalism surely would be a little outré, would it not? And yet, as one peels the onion, one can see some extraordinary connections between Gandhi and Adam Smith. In his celebrated book *The Theory of Moral Sentiments*, Smith came up with the idea of the 'impartial spectator', 'a man within the breast', which each of us creates or invents, who ends up being the judge of the moral worth of our actions. Smith makes a powerful case that 'Man naturally

desires to be loved' (Smith, 2002). Gandhi would not have agreed
to an inner categorical imperative being advocated based on the
fact that he desired to be loved by others. And Smith too takes this
approach as he moves away from merely seeking the praise of others
to seeking the praise of an imagined and imaginary spectator. Both
approaches terminate in similar consequences. Smith says: 'We soon
learn, therefore to set up in our own minds a judge between ourselves
and those we live with.' He goes on to add: 'We conceive ourselves
as acting in the presence of a person quite candid and equitable, of
one who has no particular relation, either to ourselves . . . who is
neither father, nor brother, nor friend . . . an impartial Spectator'
(Smith, 2002). The analogy between Smith's impartial spectator and
Gandhi's 'still small voice within' of conscience is uncanny (CW,
1999, v. 76, p. 349). Ironically, Gandhi would have associated this
voice not with an agnostic entity, but with the father figure of God.
The scholar Nicholas Phillipson describes Smith's impartial spectator
as follows: 'Sometimes the voice of this impartial spectator would
be judgemental, and sound like the voice of conscience or even of
the deity himself' (Phillipson, 2010). Gandhi would have concurred.
Adam Smith is seen, and rightly so, as the father of the philosophical
movement associated with modern market capitalism, commerce,
free trade, and so on. But it would be being churlish towards Smith
to suggest that he put mere material prosperity ahead of the need
for human beings to seek morally and spiritually elevating outcomes
for themselves and for others. The so-called ascetic Gandhi had this
to say about Ahmedabad, the city where he chose to live when he
returned to India from South Africa in 1915: 'There is so much
wealth in Ahmedabad that it could turn this capital of Gujarat which
is famed for its beauty into physically and spiritually the healthiest
place in India' (CW, 1999, v. 43, p. 23). The connection between
material prosperity and spiritual health could not have been better
made and would totally resonate with Smith's enduring concern with
'the most proper way of procuring wealth and abundance' (Smith,
2002). At the risk of taking on the Rudolphs, a case can be made,

however partial and indirect, that Gandhi can be seen as being an intellectual descendant not of the 'other West' but of the mainstream Scottish Enlightenment traditions of David Hume and Adam Smith. Gandhi's 'practical ethics' has a strong relationship not only to the empirical traditions of the Scots, but even to the thought processes of the celebrated English conservative philosopher Edmund Burke, himself both an admirer of Adam Smith and a respectful observer of Indian traditions (Phillipson, 2010). The point can also be made that Gandhi's Nai Talim echoed the life and achievements of that other great Scottish Enlightenment figure—the ultimate tinkering artist—James Watt.

Gandhi, the Hindu

As early as in 1921, writing in *Young India*, Gandhi said: 'I call myself a Sanatani Hindu' (CW, 1999, V. 24, P. 370). The Sanskrit expression Sanatani Hindu refers to an unbroken and timeless Hindu tradition. Till the end of his life, the Mahatma did not budge from his Hindu identity, although in his characteristic manner, he found ways to distance himself from the varnashrama-caste model by clever sleights of hand, something that has been ably analysed by the historian Nishikant Kolge (Kolge, 2017). The point that needs to be addressed is whether Hindu religious philosophy, with its aversion to materialism, can in fact be reconciled with Western traditions of market capitalism. That, of course, again depends on what one chooses to emphasize in the myriad traditions of so-called Hindu thought. For Gandhi himself, nothing highlighted mainstream Hindu 'darshana' (philosophy) better than the ancient and authoritative text Ishopanishad, or the Isavasya Upanishad. Writing in the *Harijan* in 1937, he has this to say: 'I have now come to the conclusion that if all the Upanishads and all other scriptures happened all of a sudden to be reduced to ashes, and if only the first verse of the Ishopanishad were left intact in the memory of Hindus, Hinduism would live for ever' (CW, 1999, v. 70, p. 298). Needless to say, this says more about the

effervescent Gandhi than about Hinduism. But starting with this as a
prior, let us examine Gandhi's views on 'the second and third parts' of
the first verse as he reads them. Gandhi's preference is to 'renounce'
the 'world' while enjoying it. But strangely enough, he adds the
following sentence: 'There is another rendering though: Enjoy what
He gives you.' My rudimentary Sanskrit leads me to conclude that
the verse means to say one should experience and enjoy the world/
wealth granted to us. This sentiment would, of course, have gone
down well with Smith. Gandhi and I are in the same corner with
the translation of the last part. Gandhi's version is: 'Do not covet
anybody's wealth or possession.' I would prefer 'anyone else's wealth'.
Ralph Griffith has put it thus: 'Covet no wealth of any man' (Griffith,
1987). But the net result is an emphatic defence of property rights
and the position that theft cannot be condoned. Smith would heartily
endorse such a position. The management thinker Sanjoy Mukherjee
takes the Ishopanishad one step further in aligning it with capitalist
traditions. According to him, 'The Ishopanishad says we must first
build a material foundation of life on top of which we can erect the
spiritual superstructure' (Mukherjee, 2015). Smith or Gandhi may
not have approved this neat sequential approach. Smith published his
classic text on moral philosophy, *The Theory of Moral Sentiments*, well
before his primer on capitalism, *The Wealth of Nations*. For Gandhi,
the fact that the Isavasya Upanishad opened with the statement that
'the world is pervaded by God' automatically implied that issues of
the ethics regarding wealth were secondary and derivative rather than
foundational. As it turns out, it is to Gandhi, the characteristically
most Hindu or most un-Hindu of modern Hindus, that we need to fall
back on, if we are to see one of the most seminal Indic contributions
to the evolution of modern philosophical trends.

Variegated Gandhi

While doubtless there are ways of arguing that the English common
law tenets of trusteeship can be applied to the vexing agency problem

of Smithian vintage, by asking the agent to act as a trustee with a fiduciary responsibility to the principal, it is again to Gandhi himself that we gravitate when we notice how he takes this simple idea to a larger canvas. He exhorts all rich human beings, nay, in fact all human beings, to act as 'trustees'. This goes well beyond the meticulous roles assigned to trustees in the founding documents of the Sabarmati Ashram (CW, 1999, v. 33, p. 347–348). This requires the need for a leap in how an individual views himself or herself apropos of others—and 'others' includes not just those living now, but those who are yet to be born. Writing in *Young India* in 1927, Gandhi makes a powerful statement on the nature of wealth: 'The art of amassing riches becomes a degrading and despicable art, if it is not accompanied by the nobler art of how to spend wealth usefully . . . Let not possession of wealth be synonymous with degradation, vice, and profligacy' (CW, 1999, v. 40, p. 160). A simple content analysis of this statement should include the fact that Gandhi concedes as a prior that amassing wealth is an art, and a noble one at that. It is 'useful spending' that takes it further into a 'nobler art'. The moralists in Hume and Smith might suggest that this pursuit of nobility is self-induced among human beings (Smith, 2002; Hume, 2012). The religious Gandhi presumably sees it as a God-induced obligation.

Recent developments in extensions of utilitarian economics, pioneered by George Akerlof and Rachel Kranton, suggest that the moral approaches of Smith and Gandhi can be reconciled with utilitarianism in quite unexpected ways, even though this may involve stretching the usual traditional ideas of economists to certain extremes. The 'utility' of a product, service or event refers to the pleasure or gain an individual obtains when acquiring or buying something. The concept of utility is routinely taught to students of economics. Utility, as it turns out, may also be the result of praise obtained from others. Akerlof and Kranton argue that if in fact individuals derive utility from not only being 'loved', in the Smithian sense, but also in being loved or admired vis-à-vis a particular identity, as a 'good mother' or even as a 'cool schoolchild', then much of human behaviour can be explained within this context. Needless to say, individuals respond to the identities assigned to them, thus creating a positive feedback loop for the concerned mother or child in our examples. The behavioural economist and Nobel laureate Richard Thaler has argued in favour of 'nudging' people towards certain desirable decisions. Akerlof and Kranton argue that people can be nudged towards ethical positions if we leverage their concerns about having and projecting a desired identity. Gandhi would have approved of the nudge strategy of encouraging ethical behaviour, adding in his elliptical manner that the approach be non-violent. He would have smiled and also said that while this approach was in order for others, he himself needed no nudge because he followed the dictates of his inner voice! Can Gandhi be reconciled with the well-known 'contractual' approach to agency problems pioneered by Nobel laureate Michael Jensen, his colleague William Meckling (Jensen and Meckling, 1976) and Nobel laureate Eugene Fama (Fama, 1980)? In this approach, the alignment of interests happens not on account of any overriding ethical concerns, but as a result of legal contracts among different parties, like investors, managers and lenders. This is particularly of contemporary interest, as the 2008 crisis has brought disrepute to the purely contractual approach. For Gandhi, the pursuit of utility based on identity would have made sense. His exhortations to the rich to become trustees invariably included moral homilies (from the Ishopanishad), practical anxieties (the poor may deprive you of your wealth) and nudges towards a search for approbation from others (Gandhi, 2015). Gandhi was influenced by his own idealized villager, by Christian Trappist monks, by the pedagogical pioneer Maria Montessori and by his own protégé-turned teacher J.C. Kumarappa. From these influences and from his own plastic mind, there emerged an educational philosophy centred on 'tinkering', which can be seen as Gandhi's original contribution to the field of 'Economics of Human Capital Development'. Oddly enough, the tinkering approach to education had parallels with the practical empiricist traditions symbolized by another Scottish Enlightenment figure, James Watt. There is a unique Gandhian cauldron, where we can find a whole series of extraordinarily insightful inputs for textbooks on political economy. Again, as is almost invariably the case with the Mahatma, his contributions have profound theoretical foundations and eminently practical considerations.

Methodology

The roots of Gandhi's ideas on trusteeship lie in Gujarati Bania traditions, in Hinduism (or his interpretation of Hinduism), in the ideas developed by English common law, in the Gospels, in the thoughts of the 'other Christians', the Quakers and in his own personal association with rich persons—be they Khojas, Jews or Marwaris. A strong case can be made that Gandhi and his ideas, curiously enough, fit into mainstream intellectual currents in economic thought, from Smith and Hume down to Thaler, Akerlof and Kranton. They also have linkages with Indic *purushartha* philosophical traditions. This book is devoted to exploring Gandhi's trusteeship doctrine in some detail, primarily based on textual analysis. Gandhi's central and possibly seminal work, the *Hind Swaraj*, is the starting point. I have relied heavily on Anthony Parel's edition. Parel has been very helpful to me in crossing the channel that divides the well-known political Gandhi from the lesser-known Gandhi as a thinker in the realm of political economy, and one who fundamentally re-oriented Indic thought, giving it contemporary relevance, thus fulfilling the requirements of *yuga dharma* (the virtuous conduct appropriate for the age) and propounding a moral philosophy for our times. I have analysed Gandhi's numerous articles, speeches and interviews. They are all available in the monumental *Collected Works*. While the digital edition of *Collected Works* is undoubtedly useful, I have benefited from references to direct extracts from Gandhi's writings in the *Harijan* and *Young India*, both of which were periodicals that he founded and edited. For the sources of Gandhi's ideas, I have had to enter unusual territories, like English legal history, Gujarati texts, Sanskrit scriptures, Tamil classics, Quaker tracts and the Gospels. The works of Adam Smith and the book of Akerlof and Kranton, along with the speeches of the celebrated English legal historian Frederic Maitland were key reference works. Nobel laureate Jean Tirole, with his Gallic wit, brings us back to the realms of modern economics with effortless aplomb. The Scottish historian Nicholas Phillipson's slim volume on Adam Smith was very helpful. The cross-references to David Hume and Edmund Burke were particularly illuminating. The scholar Alan Macfarlane's masterly summary of Maitland is both brilliant and magisterial. Akerlof and Kranton cogently and superbly lay out many issues associated with identity. I am grateful to Nishikant Kolge for helping me circle back to the intelligent way in which the Mahatma dealt with caste. Many of my generation are eternally grateful to the psychologist, philosopher and polymath Ashis Nandy for shooting from Gandhi's shoulder to demolish the myth of hyper-masculinity and for restoring the healing touch of androgyny. The Isavasya Upanishad, with its innumerable translations and commentaries, became obligatory reading. I had the opportunity to go back to the rare Edwin Arnold translation of the Bhagavad Gita, which Gandhi himself read almost a century and a half ago. The famous and brilliant Lloyd and Susanne Rudolph, as also the India scholar Barton Scott, provided me key insights into the mind of the enigmatic Mahatma. Gandhi was an intellectual child of the Gospels. Reading St. Mark and St. Matthew through Gandhi's lens is a special spine-chilling experience. Quaker chronicles are solid, sober and matter-of-fact, supplying a counter to the sheer romance that occupies so much of Gandhi's odyssey. The great 'Gandhian' economist J.C. Kumarappa, who writes with passion, was both Gandhi's disciple and teacher. Kumarappa has best described Gandhi's Nai Talim or New Learning programme, which I have argued as being an important contribution in the realm of the economics of human capital. Chaitra Redkar's recent (2019) book on Kumarappa was an extremely useful reference source. Ramchandra Guha's magnum opus on Gandhi arrived just as I was in the middle of writing this book. It proved very useful.

William Shirer chronicled much of the first half of the twentieth century from different vantage points. His classic work on Gandhi needs to be better known, if only for his unique and incandescent insights. He captures the spirit of the talking Gandhi, the writing Gandhi, and above all the engaging Gandhi—a human being engaged with the central human concern of how we choose to live among other human beings.

Trusteeship is a cornerstone foundational doctrine which is both many-sided and many-splendoured. Hopefully, this book will help articulate the texts such that the resulting thoughts are animated and vibrant, and equally I hope we end up invoking the Mahatma's ideas to better inform us of our economic choices in the twenty-first century as we grapple with ongoing crises in a capitalist paradigm that continues to survive and even thrive!

2

Gandhi, the English Lawyer

Barrister Gandhi

In his famous, or perhaps infamous, description of Gandhi as a half-naked fakir, Winston Churchill also described him as a 'Middle Temple' lawyer (Guha, 2018). Churchill was wrong. Gandhi was definitely a lawyer, and an English lawyer at that. But he belonged not to the Middle Temple, but to the Inner Temple. Both these so-called 'temples' were part of the four 'Inns of Court' in London, where barristers were trained. Gandhi was trained at the Inner Temple. The arcane nature of the Inns of Court, which can be thought of collectively as England's famous law university, the comic-opera costumes of 'barristers', who are different from mere lawyers, and other similar matters, can oddly enough become central to the understanding of the Mahatma and many of his seminal ideas. The eccentric English loved to have different professional categories, and in the field of law there were solicitors, advocates, counsels, barristers and so on. Given that Gandhi was going to spend most of his life as a master of the argumentative trait, it was only appropriate that he chose to become a barrister who specialized in advocacy. Gandhi became a barrister within three years of entering the Inner Temple. To use the quaint English expression, he was 'called to the Bar'. Despite his own disarming humility in his autobiography, Gandhi must have been a diligent and regular student, sitting for and passing the relevant examinations, as well as participating correctly and promptly in the unusual ritual of attending dinners, which was deemed to be the most important requirement for students of the law. Gandhi completed his studies and qualified in three years, when it was not uncommon for many students to take four years. From medieval times, the traditions of the Inns of Court, of which the Inner Temple was an integral part, required that emphasis be placed on the teaching of English common law—rather than Roman law—which remained the special field of interest for Oxford and Cambridge universities. And herein lies at least one of the key matters of importance concerning Gandhi's legal training. For 'trusteeship', which was later to emerge as central to Gandhi's ideas, remains a legal concept unique to English common law. The idea of 'trusteeship' is absent from continental systems like Code Napoleon, which is the French civil code enacted on 21 March 1804, and is still in existence, though with revisions. Trust and trusteeship are ideas that have evolved over time within the broader English concept of equity. Snell's celebrated textbook, *Equity,* was and is a must for legal students in all countries that follow the common law tradition. Gandhi knew his Snell well and makes reference to the same (CW, 1999, v. 1, p. 105). The Inner Temple itself remains, from medieval times till now, an unincorporated unorganized entity that operates 'as a trust'. It is worth thinking about the fact that Gandhi frequently exhorted his rich friends to deal with their business activities and their wealth as 'trustees' (CW, 1999, v. 93, p. 355) even if they had not set them up formally as trusts. Clearly, an entity operating as a trust was more important for the Mahatma than its formal registration as a trust.

Gandhi's Tryst with English Equity Law

Gandhi's choice of vocabulary, I would argue, is not accidental. Gandhi was acquainted with many aspects of English law. His famous, if partially apocryphal, description of Sir Stafford Cripps's proposal as a post-dated check drawn on a failing bank reveals that he was quite knowledgeable about the law of negotiable instruments, another unique Anglo-Saxon gift to the world of law and commerce. His responses to the trial judge in Ahmedabad (CW, 1999, v. 26, p. 377–386) and his 'report' on the inequities imposed on indigo farmers in Champaran (CW, 1999, v. 15, p. 366–371) show a high level of skill in legal draftsmanship. In his discussions on wealth and on the role of businesses and business owners, Gandhi could have used many words in order to express his ethical concerns: compassion, charity, inclusiveness, fairness, responsibility . . . all such words come to mind. And yet these words are conspicuously absent in Gandhi's vocabulary. Instead, the Mahatma chooses to dwell on 'trusts' and 'trusteeship'. Clearly, there was a great deal of thought that went into what in retrospect seems a simple decision in the choice of semantics. Alan Macfarlane refers to the fact that the great English historian of law and jurisprudence F.W. Maitland 'came to believe' that 'the Trust' was 'the greatest of all English legal contributions to the world' (Macfarlane, 2002). In his final years, Maitland had begun to develop ideas which were quite central among Gandhi's numerous interests and concerns. Scholar Henry Maine features on the reading list referred to by Gandhi and presumably recommended by him at the end of *Hind Swaraj* (Parel, HS, 2009). Maine had seen progress and modernity as being characterized by a movement away from status- and kinship-based societies to contractual societies, which by almost tautological definition were considered modern. It is to Maitland's credit that even while acknowledging Maine's scholarship (Maine could be seen as a precursor and guru of Maitland), he realized that the simplistic theory of so-called progressive evolution was actually contradicted both by empirical data and by the fact that creative tensions between contract, individualism and absolute equality are not resolved easily. Maitland was concerned with how Adam Smith's concepts of 'self love' and 'social love' could be harmonized, and how equality and liberty could be reconciled (Macfarlane, 2002). Gandhi's entire lifelong intellectual odyssey had almost identical concerns, even if his canvas was the Indian sub-continent, while Maitland's was medieval and modern England.

There is a unique example of unintended synchronicity in the publishing of two works by Gandhi and Maitland. We sit back and note that *Hind Swaraj* was written in 1909. The author was Gandhi, a practising Indian barrister who had been trained in the Inner Temple in London. Maitland, himself a Lincoln's Inn barrister (Lincoln's Inn being one of the other Inns of Court in London), published his brilliant work 'Equity: Equity also the Forms of Action at Common Law; Two Courses of Lectures' in the same year of 1909 (Maitland, 2011). It is almost as if, despite the distinct and distant nature of their two intellectual lives, they were pursuing similar concerns and, quite independently of each other, concluding that trust and trusteeship might hold the answer to bridging the conflict between selfishness and altruism. This conflict has been an ongoing human concern—whether in the Hindu scriptures (whose acquaintance Gandhi often made through translations by English writers), in the common wisdom of the Indian village (a romanticized version of which was clearly on Henry Maine's radar) (Maine, 2018), in the New Testament (which Gandhi frequently, almost predictably, referred to), in Adam Smith, whose 'impartial spectator' (Smith, 2002) was a figure of enduring interest for Maitland (Macfarlane, 2002), and in the very real, not-so-arcane provisions of equity in English common law. It is important to remember that Gandhi himself states that his personal religious vision, which was informed by the Bhagavad Gita, reminded him instantly of *Snell's Equity* (CW, 1999, v. 44, p. 287). Now, *Snell's Equity* is a highly prized textbook, which conspicuously lingers on the shelves of the libraries of lawyers in England and in India to this day, along with recently published annexures and appendices. And of course, the entire body of scholarship on trusts and trusteeship is derived from the English common law ideas of equity.

So, what exactly is equity, which deserved two profound lectures from Maitland (Maitland, 2011)? Equity arose in medieval England in situations where the Sovereign, acting through his Lord Chancellor, came to the conclusion that the application of strict procedures of law sometimes produces what are considered to be unjust results, and where citizens are unable to obtain suitable legal remedies. In other words, written statutes may result in legal conclusions that actually result in a perversion of justice as seen by common people; they were thus holding the common will as superior to that of arid experts. In Charles Dickens's *Oliver Twist*, a devious but half-comic character, Mr Bumble, refers to the law as an ass. One could argue that the principles of equity are required to intervene in all situations where the irrepressible Mr Bumble's argument is relevant. The Courts of Chancery, which operated separately from other courts, were specifically required to intervene in order to ensure that the principle of equity is upheld and the law does not end up behaving willy-nilly as an ass. The Courts of Chancery, therefore, acted as courts of equity to provide remedies not obtainable in the regular courts of law. Over the years, even as courts have been consolidated and procedures changed, the principle of equity has remained enshrined in all English-common-law-jurisprudence countries. The principle of equity sometimes does result in negating the letter of the law, a matter that has caused deep anxiety to continental lawyers. But this quirk has been considered a risk well worth taking in England. In his celebrated defence in the Ahmedabad court, Gandhi pleaded guilty for having violated the written law, while subtly appealing to the larger justice embedded in the principle of equity (CW, 1999, v. 26, p. 378). This seems to end up as a recurring theme in Gandhi's political activity and it, therefore, had its spillover in Gandhi's approach to economics, to wealth, to business, to capitalism, to the role of the state, to socialism, and, above all, to his need to reconcile individualism, which he was passionately committed to, with sensitivity to human comradeship and the active community of citizens. It is interesting to note that free India, which claims

Gandhi as the Father of the Nation, provides, under Article 142 of its Constitution, a discretionary power to the Supreme Court to do complete justice by projecting and enforcing the principles of equity where the texts of existing laws are deemed insufficient. The inclusion of Article 142 in the Constitution of India cannot be seen as having happened by chance. After all, the architect of India's Constitution was another England-trained barrister, B.R. Ambedkar! Trusts and trusteeship are derived from the principle of equity as distinct from the law of contracts. One can paraphrase Cassius's statement in Shakespeare's Julius Caesar: '. . . the trust, dear Brutus, is not in our contractual stars, but comes from the equity within us'—as Gandhi and Maitland independently recognized.

An ecosystem where contracts are entered into and are enforced is recognized as almost a prerequisite for what we now refer to as economic growth and development. Nobel laureate Douglas North, in his magisterial 1990 work *Institutions, Institutional Change and Economic Performance* (North, 1990), makes this case with elegance and erudition. But while contracts may be a necessary condition for orderly economic growth, equity and its first-born child, trusteeship, may hold the clue to achieving the larger goals of social freedoms and harmony. It is noteworthy to mention here that the principles of equity find their application even in contract law. For Maitland, it was important that trusts were set up by individuals and groups without the interference of the leaden hand of the state. There is no 'valuable consideration' (Maitland, 2011) when a trust is set up, unlike in the case of a contract. A trust deed contains no 'obligatory language' (Maitland, 2011). It is entirely 'voluntaristic' (Macfarlane, 2002). Ironically, there is 'detriment' to the promisee, the trustor, or the grantor of a trust (Maitland, 2011). And all of these promises and confidences are 'not enforceable by law but by equity' (Macfarlane, 2002). It is the voluntary nature of the ethic of trusteeship that Gandhi grasped and endorsed. This is what the young Gandhi has to say, well before he was accorded the honorific of Mahatma:

My study of English law came to my help. Snell's discussion of
the maxims of Equity came to my memory. I understood more
clearly in the light of the Gita teaching, the implications of the
word 'trustee'. My regard for jurisprudence increased, I discovered
it in religion. I understood the Gita teaching of non-possession to
mean that those who desired salvation should act like the trustee
who, though having control over great possessions, regards not an
iota of them as his own (CW, 1999, v. 44, p. 287).

This connection that Gandhi makes between *Snell's Equity*, the
Bhagavad Gita and trusteeship establishes once and for all the
enormous debt Gandhi owed to English common law principles
in the derivation of his ideas. It is pertinent to note that Gandhi's
personal library always included both the Gita and Snell. Gandhi's
leap from his admiration for jurisprudence to his engagement with
religion, especially an idiosyncratic interpretation of religion, is not
necessarily unusual. It was the mechanism of trusteeship that allowed
for multiple non-conformist and even anti-establishment religious
groups to flourish in England, outside the control of the state and
its Anglican establishment. Quakers, who were Gandhi's favourites
among such groups, set up trusts. And unlike joint stock companies,
these trusts needed no royal charters and they were set up precisely
to compete with the Anglican attempt at religious monopoly
(Macfarlane, 2002).

Maitland makes the case that it was the principle of equity and
the institution of the trust which enabled English citizens to form
multiple associations, thus breeding the spirit of political liberty
all around (Maitland, 2011). The French political philosopher
Alexis de Tocqueville has made a similar observation regarding
the development of civil society in America, where Anglo-Saxon
traditions of equity blossomed over time (De Tocqueville, 2003).
The continent had a different environment. In France, even 'at the
beginning of the twentieth century it was still a misdemeanor to
belong to any unauthorized association having more than twenty

members' (Macfarlane, 2002). Macfarlane makes an important point: 'The idea of a legal, unincorporated association of free people pursuing political ends was essential to democracy' (Macfarlane, 2002). And barrister Gandhi took full advantage of this right that he possessed in all parts of the British Empire. In South Africa, he set up trusts to oversee the Phoenix Settlement and Tolstoy Farm (which were community settlements established by Gandhi in Natal and Transvaal), simply by drawing up the trust deed on his own. It is certain that the racist government of that country would never have permitted the creation of these associations if they had the power to interfere. In British India, Gandhi set up trusts to conduct the affairs of his ashrams at Sabarmati and Sevagram and the Navjivan Trust to manage his numerous publishing and journalistic enterprises. When he asked his followers to boycott universities supported by the British government in India, he was able to set up non-governmental universities like the Gujarat Vidyapeeth without much difficulty. And he did all of this openly, without any need for falling back on 'secret anti-state organizations' (Macfarlane, 2002) like the triads. And, as Ashis Nandy has pointed out in a different context, Gandhi had no hesitation in challenging his imperial masters to abide by their own rules (Nandy, 2009). After all, if Oxford and Cambridge universities, as well as the Inns of Court, could operate for centuries as informal unincorporated bodies governed by the principles of equity and trusteeship, why was it necessary that universities in India had to follow Lord Dalhousie's diktat that they needed government sanction and control? Knowingly or otherwise, Gandhi was heir to an older mercantile tradition in his native Gujarat, where associative institutions like Mahajans and Nagarsheths did not need royal firmans but definitely required voluntary association. Royal firmans at best confirmed institutions decades and centuries after they were set up (Tripathi and Mehta, 1978).

Making the connection between the ways of voluntary associations and institutions in the Anglo-Saxon tradition and the similar practices among the Banias of western India could give rise to a separate book altogether. It could be argued that all of Gandhi's 'voluntary associative activities'—Phoenix Settlement, Tolstoy Farm, Sabarmati Ashram, Navjivan Press, Gujarat Vidyapeeth, etc.—were perforce voluntary and outside state control, because he was in his lifetime perpetually a leader in opposition to the state and therefore was unlikely to receive state support. This argument, however, misses something fundamental about Gandhi's approach. Even during the years when his fellow Congress party persons were in power in several provinces and for the few months that he lived after Indian independence, Gandhi sought no state support for his activities, although he could have easily accessed such support. His consequentialist argument would have been that state support would have involved the intrusion of a deadening hand and an elimination of free creativity or meaningful constructive activity. His moral argument would have been that state support would destroy the agency of the 'trustees', who were duty-bound to pursue their roles and actions on their own and not be forced by state coercion or tempted by state subsidy. It is worth thinking about whether India's rich would have been better legatees of their country if they had, after Independence, followed Gandhi's voluntary vision rather than become dependent on state handouts. Both the British Raj and the government of free India have chosen a top-down state-sponsored approach. It is as if the senior functionaries of the independent Indian state ended up being good disciples of Dalhousie. Today one would need state approval to establish a Gujarat Vidyapeeth. Needless to say, this is far from Gandhi's vision—the vision adopted by his Gujarati Bania forebears and, ironically, by his English law teachers in their own country, but usually forgotten in their imperial possessions.

Individualist Gandhi

The German historian Dieter Rothermund has emphasized that Gandhi repeatedly went on record opposing the intrusive state that violates the property rights of individuals (Rothermund, 1992). How then was Gandhi to square the circle in attempting to work for the welfare of the poor? He was practical enough to understand that appealing to the rich in the words of the Gita or the New Testament may not be sufficient. He therefore appealed to them in consequentialist terms. The rich ran the risk of being attacked and dispossessed by the more numerous poor (CW, 1999, v. 48, p. 53–54). The rich were personally likely to be cursing rather than helping their progeny by giving them large legacies (CW, 1999, v. 82, p. 63). He therefore saw the trust as a voluntary route for the rich to deal with their practical problems. He also saw trusteeship as a system of checks and balances for a business, where capital, labour and customers kept checks on each other (CW, 1999, v. 73, p. 253). The introduction of the customer as a third side to this new tripod, which replaced the traditional capital–labour stand-off, has to be one of the Mahatma's most impressive and underestimated insights. Today it is common in business literature to talk of the written and unwritten contracts between businesses and customers. To go beyond contracts and to think of a tripartite relationship based on equity and trust may very well be the next milestone that needs to be crossed.

Despite the fact that the principles of equity are applicable to contract law, it is not an accident that there remains a big gulf between the practice of contract and equity. It could be argued in a strict contractual world, where the customer needs to beware, that the business fulfils its part of the contract when the good or service has been provided. An interesting question can be raised—as to whether it is more appropriate to ask of the business if, going beyond the limited contract, the customer is actually satisfied or even delighted by the transaction. This would be an appropriate application of the principles of equity and of Gandhi's worldview, as demonstrated in his astonishingly prescient inclusion of customers in the business tripod. Clearly, both theoretical and empirical research can be pursued in this area. In empirical and consequentialist terms, can we find evidence that this approach leads over time to greater value creation for the business? In theoretical terms, does this approach not endow business with a higher moral purpose and remove some, if not much, of the stigma associated in the popular mind of the greedy businessperson who is oblivious to the greater good of society?

It must be noted that for himself, Gandhi never required a consequentialist excuse. He was, after all, a religious person immersed in the Isavasya Upanishad and the New Testament. It is fascinating to note that Gandhi willed the copyright on his works to Navjivan Trust—a trust which by its very name is committed to the creation of a new life for all humans, a life touched by erudite jurisprudence and a sense of the sacred, or shall we just say a quaint combination of Snell and the Gita. A trust is an intuitive rather than a textual legal concept. It is voluntary. It rests on a promise and a sense of obligation rather than on a transaction and a consideration. The courts enforce the provisions of a trust not because the sovereign so commands them. The courts are guided by the fact that the grantor of a trust has expressed a confidence that his or her wishes will be considered a 'sacred trust' by society at large. And as this idea grows, it can encompass many fields of human endeavour.

Gandhi found the greatest use of the trusteeship doctrine in the political field, as he repeatedly addressed the issue that the British had failed by their own standards of trusteeship. Even in the late 1700s, the English philosopher and statesman Edmund Burke had argued against the arbitrary high-handedness of the East India Company, a selfish mercantile corporation that managed to make itself the ruler of a large country (Mukherjee, 2005). Adam Smith was completely opposed to the idea of having a commercial organization govern a country and its people (Phillipson, 2010). Maitland had maintained that 'the Herrschaft which the East India Company had acquired in India was held "in trust" for the Crown of Great Britain', and 'the whole of the British Empire came to be seen as held "in trust" for the peoples themselves' (Macfarlane, 2002).

When he turned up in London for the Round Table Conference, Gandhi made out the case for the failure of the British in their fiduciary duties as a trustee with an astonishing brilliance (Shirer, 1980). Gandhi was quite clear that when India became free it would honour its debts, because it was the honourable thing to do. But those debts that the trustee, the British rulers, had incurred for their benefit or whim and then saddled on to the Indian fisc, could not be and should not be honoured by India. They should be borne by Britain. William Shirer, who was witness to Gandhi's marvellous extempore speech, noted that many of the hard-core British supporters of imperialism in the audience were stunned by the clarity and intensity of this Gujarati Bania barrister, who simultaneously offended and astonished them (Shirer, 1980). Gandhi's case regarding the fiduciary duties of a trustee was made not with the British alone in mind. After Indian independence, Gandhi was adamant that the Indian government had no moral, legal or Constitutional right to hang on to the funds which were held on Pakistan's behalf by India as a trustee. Many Indians, including the Mahatma's assassin, were appalled by this stance (Guha, 2018). One can only conclude that they were not privy to the ideas of Snell, Maitland and the Gita as Gandhi understood them.

As the English escaped from the tyrannies of the divine right of kings and of a state religion, Maitland maintained that it was 'easier' to think of the English sovereign as a 'trustee for his people' and not as an 'officer, official functionary or even first magistrate' (Macfarlane, 2002). Gandhi endorsed this view completely. He viewed the British governor general in India as the country's 'first servant', and strongly recommended that Lord Mountbatten should be succeeded by a young woman of impeccable character who happened to be a resident of an untouchable shanty in Delhi (CW, 1999, v. 95, p. 347–348). Everyone was amused by the Mahatma's extraordinary sense of humour and irony, everyone other than perhaps Lord Mountbatten. But we cannot and must not forget that even in his humorous moments, Gandhi radiated a special wisdom. The fact of the matter is that if you or I started a trust for the benefit of our descendants, we would first and foremost pay attention to the moral character of the trustee, who is expected to behave honourably but may very well fall short of this expectation. Heraclitus is supposed to have said, 'character is destiny'. The historian Dipesh Chakravarty has argued that Gandhi's contemporary, the eminent historian Jadunath Sircar, attached the greatest of importance to character in the development of history (Chakrabarty, 2015). Even as he semi-humorously recommends an untouchable girl of impeccable character for the highest office in India, Gandhi seems to be telling us that in the absence of a commitment to a moral imperative, human activity in economic, political and other spheres will resemble empty husks.

3

Bania Gandhi*

Gandhi and Ahmedabad

Barrister Gandhi has not yet been fully transformed into Mahatma Gandhi. By 1915, he has returned from South Africa. He has travelled a bit in India. Now he must choose a place to settle down, a place where he can put down his roots. He has returned to the land of his birth—but Porbandar in Kathiawar is not an attractive option. By now Gandhi has embraced politics as his passion. And the liberation or 'Swaraj' of India is central to that passion. Is not his seminal work called *Hind Swaraj* or 'Indian Freedom'? In his foreword to Gokhale's speeches, Gandhi says this about the Indian society of his times: 'To be sure, we cannot rise again till our political conditions change for the better' (Parel, HS, 2009). But can Gandhi be a politician in Kathiawar? The British strategy of ruling through an Indian intermediary puppet-prince trips up the ambitious barrister. In Kathiawar, any oppositional politics will be seen as opposition to an Indian ruler, not to the foreign ruler who

---

* A shortened, summarized variant of this chapter has been converted into a standalone paper jointly authored by Shishir Jha and myself, and has been published in the *Economic and Political Weekly*.

controls the puppet. Gandhi is also quite aware that political rights are more respected in those parts of India directly administered by the British than in princedoms as in Kathiawar. So he needs to find the right place. Gandhi observes that Gokhale 'firmly declared that unless our political movement was informed by the spirit of dharma, it would be barren' (Parel, HS, 2009). There Gandhi is fairly early in the game tying up the 'Hindu canonical aims of life', as Anthony Parel would call the purusharthas. Parel argues that for Gandhi, 'artha' is more than just pursuit of wealth or pursuit of power. It is about economics and politics as human activities— and for us a convenient way to engage with Gandhi's political economy (Parel, 2006). This argument is covered in some detail in Chapter 8. And Gandhi is emphatic that 'artha' which is not intertwined with dharma (virtue, righteousness, ethical conduct) is 'barren', as his own political guru Gokhale had pointed out (Parel, HS, 2009) So, how does Gandhi find the right place in British India to settle down? Being in Gujarat is helpful to him as he is a Gujarati, after all. Bombay is a heavily Gujarati town and there are many supporters of Gandhi and of 'swaraj' there. There is also Surat as a possibility. But he chose Ahmedabad. And therein lies a story. Here is a quote from Gandhi just around the time he moves into Ahmedabad: 'If the wealthy and the educated wish, they can change the face of Ahmedabad. The biggest Jain firm is in Ahmedabad. It is said that the firm of Anandji Kalyanji is wealthier than any other firm in the world which can be described as a religious body' (CW, 1999, v. 43, p. 23). This unexpected sentence sent me off on multiple journeys exploring a uniquely Indian, nay Gujarati, wellspring from where the Mahatma seems to have drawn considerable inspiration. I explored the world of Gujarati 'pedhis' and 'nagarsheths' and found empirical 'goodies' in the work of Dwijendra Tripathi and M.J. Mehta (Tripathi and Mehta, 1978). And I found a theoretical paradigm where I could locate the Mahatma's intellectual forebears in an authentically Indian setting as I explored *The Work of Theory: Thinking Across*

Traditions, by Prathama Banerjee, Aditya Nigam and Rakesh Pandey (Banerjee, Nigam, and Pandey, 2016).

The Anandji Kalyanji Trust

The Anandji Kalyanji Trust, as it is known today, became a formal legal 'trust' under the new colonial laws of the late nineteenth century. Before that, for possibly two or three centuries, it was known as Anandji Kalyanji Pedhi. The Gujarati word 'pedhi' is loosely translated as 'firm'. In actuality, in substance, this 'pedhi' operated pretty much as a modern common law trust does. The principal activity of the Anandji Kalyanji Trust is the maintenance and upkeep of several important Jain temples. The aesthetically important Ranakpur temple in Rajasthan is one of them. In conversation with the head of the Anandji Kalyanji Trust, Samveg Lalbhai, in 2013, I ran into a unique interpretation of legal and beneficial ownership of property as well as an understanding of trusteeship obligations. From Lalbhai's perspective, the Ranakpur temple does not belong to the Trust. In fact, the temple and the properties surrounding the temple belong, according to Lalbhai, to the resident Deity—Lord Adinath. The trustees are responsible for 'managing' the finances of the Deity and ensuring the upkeep and maintenance of the temple—all on behalf of the Deity.

The idea of acting on behalf of the Deity is a hoary one. The earliest reference may be in Valmiki's epic, the Ramayana, when Bharata places his brother Rama's sandals on the throne, and sits on the floor to rule the kingdom on behalf of his brother. Rama is absent, but present through his footwear, just as the divine Neminatha is present through his idol in Ranakpur. In the 1700s, the Travancore chieftain Marthanda Varma took this one step forward when he handed over his southern Indian kingdom permanently to Vishnu, as represented by the Padmanabha idol in the Anantapadmanabhaswamy temple in Thiruvananthapuram. While Bharata and Marthanda Varma may have done it in order to establish a sense of legitimacy in the eyes of their subjects, in the case of the trustees of the Anandji Kalyanji Trust, they simply have no role or right to existence if there were no Deity, whose service (including the required worship rituals) is their sole raison d'être.

This brings me almost effortlessly and instinctively to Banerjee et al., who explore and reject the powerful and power-laden intellectual paradigm that all philosophical positions are primarily derived from Western theory or theories, with at best a quaint non-Western topping added to the dish—e.g., viewing Indian philosophical and legal ideas as a supplement to English legal and Christian traditions, from where Gandhi supposedly derived his primary ideas. According to them, the trap Indians have repeatedly fallen into is that 'we believe that we cannot do without Western concepts'. At best our contribution lies in giving these Western concepts 'new content and new contours' (Banerjee, Nigam and Pandey, 2016). And this is precisely what I believe can be actually rejected and the counter established—that a very significant source of Gandhi's ideas on trusteeship is distinctly Indian and simply does not fall into the Western/non-Western, metropolitan/provincial, central/peripheral binary modes. It is interesting that the sentence immediately preceding Gandhi's reference to the Anandji Kalyanji Trust reads as follows: 'If the wealthy and the educated wish, they can change the face of Ahmedabad' (CW, 1999, v. 43, p. 23). Following this, Gandhi seems to be pointing out to these 'wealthy and educated folks' that there exists in their own backyard a fine example of trusteeship, which can help us build theoretical frameworks as well as take practical organizational measures that can help us address the problem of how to use wealth to 'change the face' (CW, 1999, v. 43, p. 23) of our cities, presumably for the better—not insignificant objective in any discourse on political economy.

The Anandji Kalyanji Trust, says its own website, goes back to the 1600s, and certainly records are available from the 1700s, a good hundred years before the British conquest of Gujarat. The Gujarati work *Sheth Anandji Kalyanji Pedhino Itihaas* establishes quite clearly that the traditions of the Trust, including issues such as prevention of misuse of office by trustees, ensuring the orderly succession of trustees, the undertaking of new projects which, while keeping with the spirit of the original intentions of the pedhi, ended up exploring new areas and activities—all evolved independent of any Western influence, theoretical or practical. The idea that each individual deity in a temple was the owner of the related properties placed significant restrictions on commingling funds between temples (deities). The application of this intelligent, even fictionalized idea (that is, if you happen to subscribe to the view that deities are fictional entities) to the vexed issue of fiduciary fund management faced (and sometimes evaded) by modern fund managers did not escape me. One of the problems that the current head of the Trust, Samveg Lalbhai, and his fellow-trustees grapple with is that the funds, which belong to the Deity, can only be used for the Deity——for rituals, for maintenance of the temple, for buying jewels and ornaments for the deity. These funds cannot be used, for instance, for feeding or otherwise helping visiting pilgrims. For such activities, funds need to be raised quite separately. Once again, the obvious parallel between this constraint and the modern financial market covenants on 'use of funds', which are increasingly mandated by regulation, did not escape me.

The interesting thing is that the 'pedhi', which had existed for a couple of centuries, decided in the late 1800s, with the advent and firm establishment of the rule of new masters, that it made sense to adopt the nomenclature most appropriate apropos of the new dispensation. The 'pedhi' could be too easily confused with a firm or company. The new rulers and their judges had their own vocabulary. Why not leverage their vocabulary and become a 'trust', something that they would understand? Going back to Banerjee et al., it is important to understand that the persons behind the pedhi, now the trust, by agreeing to write up a 'trust deed', as the new common law ecosystem demanded, did not at any stage concede that from their perspective each temple belonged to this new-fangled institution. The rightful owner remained the deity ensconced within, something that their new rulers would not have understood, let alone appreciated. Converting the pedhi into a trust must be seen both as a pragmatic act to suit the new situation and a very creative solution to the issue of how exactly the deities were going to be propitiated and the temples managed in the new era. To the credit of the new rulers, they admitted after some convolutions that deities could be 'legal persons'—that expression being part of the legal 'fictions' of the English. In the celebrated 1925 case of Pramath Nath Mullick versus Pradyumna Kumar Mullick, the British Indian court ruled that a Deity/Idol is a 'juristic entity' (Bombay High Court, 1925). Banerjee et al. would have a field day arguing whether in this case it was English common law that benefited from the Indian 'theory' (remember, it goes all the way back to Valmiki's epic) or whether it was 'Indian knowledge' that got added to a dominant Western theory as 'deviant histories'. Another case, that of Shri Thakur Radhavallabhji, is also of great interest. It pertained to the question of who could sue the 'trustee/trustees' on behalf of the Deity. Now the judiciary of independent India came up with an interesting way out. They ruled that a 'devotee', in this case Bishwanath, who is a presumed 'spiritual beneficiary' of the Deity, could sue on the Deity's behalf (Supreme Court of India, 1967).

This must have had a sobering effect on the Anandji Kalyanji trustees—just knowing that an offended pilgrim, a 'spiritual beneficiary' of the Deity, could sue on behalf of the Deity! A couple of asides: in independent India, the State of Bihar wanted to grab lands from deities. In the case of Ramjanakijee Deities versus the State of Bihar, the government argued that all lands controlled by a trust were one piece of property and therefore subject to land ceiling laws as such. The Supreme Court ruled in favour of two separate Deities as juristic entities, and held that the trustees simply managed two sets of properties on behalf of two different persons with separate property rights (Supreme Court of India, 1999). The irony of the modern (or should we call it the post-modern) tendency has been the taxman's attack on deities. But of course, even deities, who are deathless and immortal, are subject to taxes. In Jogendra Nath Naskar versus the Commissioner of Income Taxes, with the consistency required in terms of the common law principle of following precedents, the courts of independent India ruled that a Deity/Idol is a juristic entity, both capable of and obliged to pay taxes, like any other person (Calcutta High Court, 1963). The ultimate vindication of the principle that knowledge/theory is not universally Western, with add-ons from other cultures or civilizations, comes from the fact that four decades after the British had left India, an English judge ruled in the case of the Pathur Nataraja (an Idol/Deity stolen from India) that the said Nataraja was a juristic person. The court of appeal as well as the House of Lords upheld this position (the all-England Law Reports, 1991). This helped the Indian government immensely in getting back a stolen statue—sorry, Deity/Idol/Person! In the recent Ayodhya judgement, the Supreme Court of India accepted the argument of the noted lawyer K. Parasaran that Lord Rama was a juristic person (SCI, 2019). The intertwining of Indian and English legal traditions is complete, and the very question as to which one is derivative becomes irrelevant.

Persistent Gujarati Traditions

The German sociologist Max Weber is universally regarded as the pioneering scholar who analysed the birth and the growth of modern capitalism. Weber has argued that the accelerated growth of capitalism in northern Europe, and later in North America, had much to do with the growth of Protestant religious traditions. Weber posits the existence of a 'Protestant ethic', which stressed sobriety rather than ostentatious display of wealth, which encouraged wealth creation, which viewed wealth as instrumental means to larger religious ends. Weber has argued that the absence of such an ethic prevented societies like India from developing indigenous capitalist traditions (Weber, 2006). Today, one can safely say that Weber was deeply mistaken. The historian Chhaya Goswami, in her book on Kacchhi traders (Goswami, 2016), proves Weber wrong. She makes the important point that the Kacchhis had a well-developed system of cross-border capitalism (globalization?)—encompassing insurance, marine insurance, foreign exchange trading, bills of exchange—even before the time period assigned to the foundations of Western capitalism by Max Weber. And yet, whenever any of us discuss Indian ocean economic history, we are tempted to try and fit it into a Weberian paradigm, or if we are more eclectic, a Braudelian world view (Braudel being the great French historian of Western capitalism) (Braudel, 1992), raising the shackles of Banerjee et al., and correctly so. Goswami makes the case that Mahajans (we need not say that Mahajans are similar to Western guilds. We can quite easily say that guilds are Western variants of Mahajans) and Nagarsheths were common not only in central Gujarat but also in outlying Kacchh (Goswami, 2016). In 1978, Dwijendra Tripathi and M.J. Mehta wrote an often-ignored paper on the Nagarsheths of Ahmedabad, which is of intense interest to anyone trying to figure out where Gandhi got some, if not many, of his ideas. They start by making the case that 'the traditional division of Indian history into ancient, medieval, and modern periods . . . has positively hampered a proper understanding of the evolution of social institutions' (Tripathi and Mehta, 1978). One could add that the excessive focus on Sanskrit texts following Sir William Jones's example, along with the rigid idea of periodization, has led to a poorer understanding not only of social institutions, but also of ideas in the realm of the humanities. The traveller Nicholas Downtown, who visited Ahmedabad in 1615, described the buzzing mercantile centre as a veritable 'confluence of most nations of the world'. Tripathi and Mehta have this to say: '. . . the merchants immigrating into the city from other cities in Gujarat and other parts of the country brought with them the tradition of Mahajans and this institution took firm roots in Ahmedabad at a very early stage.' The historians R.C. Mujumdar, A.S. Altekar and others have talked about the 'headman of a guild' in so-called ancient India being referred to as a '*shresthin*'.

Uncannily, the word '*shreshta*' finds mention in a sale deed or '*khatapatra*' in 1627, suggesting that the institution never quite fully di*sa*ppeared, as the ancient-medieval binary would imply. A 'Moghul firman' or imperial order from 1644 also refers to 'Mahajans', clearly suggesting that the institution 'had been in existence for quite some time' (Tripathi and Mehta, 1978). Tripathi and Mehta painstakingly establish the case that among the 'shreshtas' of different 'Mahajans', the 'nagarsheth' emerged, at least in Ahmedabad, as the first among equals, by an organic process of popular consent (Tripathi and Mehta, 1978). They contest the view of Maganlal Vatakchand in his classical history of Ahmedabad (*Amdavadno Itihas*), where he argued that the institution originated with the conferment of the title on the celebrated Shantidas Jhaveri by an imperial Moghul firman issued by the emperor Jahangir. Based on a review of the documents available with Shantidas's descendants and elsewhere, Tripathi and Mehta conclude that in fact Shantidas himself never possessed this title, but the title gradually accreted to his descendants after Shantidas's death. Other merchants contested the title itself, even as Shantidas's brother began its usage, in part as being the successor to Shantidas's mantle as the pre-eminent merchant of Ahmedabad. It eventually got formally 'conferred' on Shantidas's grandson Khushalchand in 1724, after 'he paid a huge amount as ransom to the city's invaders from his personal pocket'. Commissariat in his history of Gujarat mentions that after the magnanimous rescue of their city, 'all the Mahajans of the city of Ahmedabad', representing different communities and trades, resolved that henceforth Khushalchand and his descendants would receive in perpetuity a levy of a quarter per cent on all goods stamped in the municipal weighing yard. The title was conferred by popular acclaim, not by royal decree. After this incident, the venerable *Mirat-I-Ahmadi*, a history of Gujarat in Persian, almost invariably refers to Khushalchand as 'Nagarsheth'. Tripathi and Mehta go on to describe how this new title attracted other rivals. After a prolonged period, the Jhaveri family got it on a hereditary basis, now not just by popular acclaim, but backed by a formal imperial charter (Tripathi and Mehta, 1978).

What Gandhi Took from Ahmedabad

The key learning from this exploration of Ahmedabad's business history is that social institutions like the Mahajans and the Nagarsheths seem to have had an amazing continuity across rigid periods of history (the rigidity being in the eyes of the beholder rather than in the historical events themselves) and that the 'theoretical framework' that Banerjee et al. posit, which is simultaneously Indian and universal, can arise from the actual workings of these social institutions. Some of the nuances of these theories are waiting for those who have eyes to read the humble Gujarati khaatapatras, not just Latin-laden common law case histories or William Jonesian Sanskrit texts, which can be safely consigned to the realm of the antique, the quaint and the exotic. Gandhi had a special love for Ahmedabad and a strong association with Ahmedabad's Bania community. As mentioned earlier, Gandhi, on one occasion, said: 'There is so much wealth in Ahmedabad that it could turn this capital of Gujarat which is famed for its beauty into physically and spiritually the healthiest place in India' (CW, 1999, v. 43, p. 23). Paying tribute to one of Ahmedabad's richest men and philanthropists, Gandhi said, 'I sincerely wish that the good rich men of the city take forward Chinubhai's legacy and contribute to social causes and towards moral upkeep of society. I have no doubt that Ahmedabad will set an example for the whole country and even the world' (John, 2018). One can clearly see the Amdavadi roots of the Mahatma's future exegeses on the subject of trusteeship. Content-analysing these two statements, which on their own seem to be stray pleasantries, one is struck by so many important nuances. First of all, the existence of 'so much wealth' is automatically assumed to be a good thing. But almost immediately there follows the observation on the instrumental nature of its goodness. Great wealth will eventually be acknowledged as good, provided it could make the city 'physically and spiritually' healthy. The Mahatma, as ever, is obsessed with cleanliness and sanitation. One needs only pay attention to the mention of 'physical health', which, incidentally, preceded spiritual health. And what about the expected role of 'good rich men' (presumably different from bad rich men!)? Again, they need to see their wealth as not being important by itself and acquiring importance only if used properly. In other words, wealth has instrumental rather than intrinsic value. And the rich need to contribute to 'social causes and moral upkeep of society'. At least here there is no intrinsic suspicion of wealth, which occasionally does crop up in other writings of Gandhi's. And there is a strong appreciation that wealth is desirable, perhaps even necessary, for physical, spiritual and moral health. Lastly, the universal aim of so many of Gandhi's thoughts and actions comes through incandescently, when he mentions that Ahmedabad could and should set an example to the whole world.

Alternative Lineage

The intellectual lineages seem complex, but are actually quite simple. The Gujarati Bania had a 'trusteeship' tradition of great antiquity, probably one that has been unbroken in some ways even from remote antiquity (Tripathi and Mehta, 1978). That they used words like mahajan and not 'guild', nagarsheth instead of the tongue-twisting 'prominent merchant leader, leading citizen and philanthropist of the city', that their two century-old trust was known as a 'pedhi'—all these do not in any way diminish their importance or salience. The fact that even in his times Gandhi met shreshtis, who could be considered embodiments of this tradition, is also of great significance. Gandhi singles out the Jain Anandji Kalyanji Trust for mention. The head of this trust for five decades was the renowned Kasturbhai Lalbhai, a direct descendant of the renowned Shantidas Jhaveri and Nagarsheth Khushalchand (Desai, 1983). It is well known that the Mahatma was very friendly with

Kasturbhai and spent considerable time in engaging with him. Kasturbhai's views on trusteeship from his own perspective needed no shelter within the domains of dominant/metropolitan/Western theoretical paradigms. He could fall back on his ancestral belief that the temple's properties belonged to the Deity ensconced therein and that his own duty lay in managing the properties well. The fact that the Deity's funds could not be diverted to concerns other than the Deity's own ones pointed to a restriction on diversion of funds, representing a Gujarati precursor to the expression 'fiduciary' duty, with all its Latin connotations. Kasturbhai was certainly intensely aware of his duties as a descendant and successor of the distinguished Nagarsheth Khushalchand, who at personal cost saved his city from plunder. Kasturbhai's own contributions to the civic landscape of Ahmedabad are legion. Kasturbhai himself devoted considerable amount of time and energy grappling with what we would today refer to as succession and corporate governance issues. A descendant of Shantidas Jhaveri traditionally chaired the trust. According to the present head of the trust, Samveg Lalbhai, Kasturbhai was very worried that a future descendant of his may be literally unworthy of the position and the Trust. So he had the rules of succession amended in order to take this possibility into account. The other element that doubtless impressed the Mahatma was the intense practicality of the Gujarati Bania traditions. For example, where necessary and appropriate, a Moghul firman was sought and obtained. And once the British rulers had established themselves, the Anandji Kalyanji Pedhi formally converted itself into a 'trust' under the new colonial laws late in the nineteenth century. However, neither of these acts implies that the institution or the activities derived from Moghul or British traditions. In some sense the Deity still ruled, and if some British judges reluctantly conceded that the Deity was this quaint, new, exotic thing known as a juristic entity, then the new rulers were simply falling in line with an old tradition, making the case for the universality of human ideas, something which Gandhi would have embraced, but something which would have been dismissed by the German philosopher Hegel, who had a condescending attitude towards Indian history and Indian philosophy (Rathore and Mohapatra, 2017).

Trusteeship represents a significant, and in some ways a uniquely Gandhian, insight into a variety of vexed problems that all students of political economy are sooner or later forced to confront. Gandhi's insights have universal validity, and in some respects may be very useful in the current discourse on agency problems, corporate governance, corporate social responsibility, wealth management, philanthropy, and so on. Gandhi, as a citizen of the world, had different sources for his ideas—to all of which he added his own passionate intensity. But in seeking these sources, it would do well for us to remember that a great deal was owed by him to the intellectual traditions and actual practices of Gujarati Banias. After all, as Rajni Bakshi points out, Gandhi was quite proud to refer to himself as a '*vanika putra*', son of a Bania (Bakshi, 2012).

4

Gandhi and the Christian Message

The 1916 Allahabad Speech: Gandhi's Love for the Gospels

We need to again consider the crucial period less than a decade after the publication of *Hind Swaraj*. The barrister from South Africa is back in India and is exploring his native country following the advice of his political guru, Gokhale. On 22 December 1916, Gandhi delivers a lecture at a meeting of the Muir Central College Economic Society in Allahabad. The title of the lecture is: 'Does economic progress clash with real progress?' (Parel, HS, 2009; CW 1999, v. 15, pp. 272 and 274). The great Gandhian scholar Anthony Parel has included the full text of this astonishing speech in his edition of a book that includes the *Hind Swaraj* and several other crucial writings of Gandhi. Parel has this to say about the speech in his short introductory note: 'It contains Gandhi's basic ideas on economic development. Note its wide intellectual culture, quoting as it were in one breath the New Testament, Shakespeare and A.R. Wallace, the co-discoverer with Darwin of the principle of natural selection' (Parel, HS, 2009). Parel is absolutely correct when he mentions that this lecture contains Gandhi's 'basic ideas on economic development'. While Gandhi's ideas kept evolving over the next three decades, his basic political economy formulations were in place along with *Hind Swaraj* (1909) and this lecture in 1916. In the short editor's note, Parel makes reference to the lecture's 'wide intellectual culture'. While this is undoubtedly impressive, what emerges as unexpectedly stunning is that the lecture turns out to be almost a Christian manifesto based on the Gospels. Mathew and Mark are quoted extensively, and Jesus is hailed as the 'greatest economist of his time' (Parel, HS, 2009; CW, 1999, v. 15, p. 275). Someone who reads this alone could, with good reason, conclude that all of Gandhi's economic ideas and insights are quite simply distillations of the Gospels.

Gandhi's opening salvo consists of a loud admission that he has not read Mill, Marshall or Adam Smith. And he uses Christian vocabulary, calling himself 'a sinner past redemption' in refusing to heed the advice given to him to read up these worthies. But it should not escape our attention that in preparing for his lecture to the College Economics Society, he has made sure that he is at least acquainted with the names of important economists, including Alfred Marshall, who was of relatively recent vintage and who is considered a father figure in the field of microeconomics. Right up front, Gandhi deftly addresses what to him represents a clever misrepresentation that somehow religion or morality have a great love for extreme poverty. He refers to 30 million Indians (the population of India at that time was 318 million) 'living on one meal a day'. Gandhi sets up an imaginary set of opponents to his own position—'they'. Apparently, 'they' are of the opinion that 'before we can think or talk of the moral welfare' of these famished 30 million, we 'must satisfy their daily wants. With these, they say material progress spells moral progress' (Parel, HS, 2009; CW 1999, v. 15, p. 274). Up to this point, Gandhi seems to have no great disagreement with the rather clever and loud 'they'. In a sense, 'they' are only reformulating and echoing the view Vivekananda enunciated in the nineteenth century—that to discuss religion, spirituality and morality with a 'starving person' is both inappropriate and insulting. Vivekananda was making his own case for economic progress as a prerequisite for matters concerning the spirit (Vivekananda and Nikhilananda, 1953). But the next step of 'their' argument, as Gandhi imagines it, simply will not do. 'And then is taken a sudden jump: what is true of thirty millions is true of the universe.' And now enters lawyer Gandhi. 'They' apparently have not been to law school. 'They forget that hard cases make bad law.' Now the lawyer in Gandhi is angry. So he goes on to say: 'I need hardly say to you how ludicrously absurd this deduction would be' (Parel, HS, 2009; CW 1999, v. 15, p. 274). But all of these are still in the realm of lawyerly arguments. And Gandhi seems to instinctively realize that they will not do, or at least they will not be enough. Time and again, the so-called moralists lose the argument against the so-called economists because poverty ends up looking like something that the moralists love, but it is something which violates human dignity so profoundly that moralists, at least the poverty-loving ones, are bound to lose the argument. The next statement is absolutely central to the Mahatma's position. It is acutely informed by the empirical reality of his country in his lifetime. 'No one has ever suggested that grinding pauperism can lead to anything else than moral degradation' (Parel, HS, 2009; CW, 1999, v. 15, p. 274).

Many of Gandhi's critics have argued that he romanticized poverty. And yet this one statement of his proves how wrong they were and are. Whatever else religion in general and Christianity in particular may have done to Gandhi, a romanticized love for 'grinding pauperism' was not on the cards. Statisticians have a way of describing extremes. They talk of the data being more than two standard deviations away from the mean in normal distributions. Neither is Gandhi, and nor are we, talking about extreme poverty. We are talking about the ordinary realm. And once again the Mahatma defines it with an uncanny and brilliant insight: 'Every human being has a right to live and therefore to find the wherewithal to feed himself and where necessary to clothe and house himself' (Parel, HS, 2009; CW, 1999, v. 15, p. 274). If you cannot feed, clothe and house yourself decently, you are definitely several standard deviations away from the normal mean. That level of material prosperity is what Gandhi would enunciate as normal. In the India of 1916, with its enormous poverty, advocating that limited normality might of course have appeared to suggest a communist manifesto vision of the world! From there, our unpredictable Mahatma switches gears and reminds us that 'Take no thought for the morrow' is an injunction from the Gospel of St. Matthew, which he finds as central to 'almost all the religious scriptures of the world'. The conundrum is a tough one indeed, especially if one is not particularly poor, but lays claim to affection for or connection with the poor. Gandhi never shies away from the simple-sounding but excruciatingly difficult questions.

The Mahatma extricates himself from his self-imposed difficult predicament in front of the Allahabad students by falling back on the Gospels all over again. He switches from Matthew to Mark. We are not talking now of a casual saviour, or one with a sense of humour. According to the Mahatma: 'Jesus is in his solemn mood; he is earnest. He talks of eternity. He knows the world about him' (Parel, HS, 2009; CW 1999, v. 15, p. 275). This portion of the speech is long, complicated, and full of both Gospel quotations and Gandhi's interjections. Interestingly, it ends as follows: "'How hardly shall they that have riches enter into the kingdom of God? It is easier for a camel to go through the eye of a needle than for a rich man to enter into the kingdom of God!'" And now, for Gandhi's elaboration: 'Here you have an eternal rule of life stated in the noblest words the English language is capable of producing' (Parel, HS, 2009; CW, 1999, v. 15, p. 276). Suddenly we are face to face with someone who loves the King James Bible not only because its content poetically resonates within him, but also because its language more prosaically grips him. Gandhi never surprises with his unorthodoxy, his eccentricity and, at the end of the day, the resplendent nature of his insights. He goes on to assure his audiences that 'I will not insult you by quoting in support of the law stated by Jesus passages from writings and sayings of our own sages, passages even stronger if possible than the Biblical extracts I have drawn your attention to' (Parel, HS, 2009; CW 1999, v. 15, p. 276). Now, to use a modern expression, the Mahatma is swimming in glue. And yet, like so many other dilemmas that he has to deal with, this too is one where he will try his best to juggle and keep many balls in the air. Just consider this sentence: 'We should still have, as we have always had, in our midst people who make the pursuit of wealth their aim in life,' (Parel, HS, 2009; CW 1999, v. 15, p. 277). One wonders if Gandhi bothered to realize, let alone appreciate, the excruciating decisions he imposed on his businessmen-'supporters' like G.D. Birla or even harder decisions on his businessmen-'followers' like Jamnalal Bajaj (Jones and Kiron, 2017). At least the poor can pursue the wherewithal to feed, clothe and house themselves. What are the rich supposed to do in order to meet the difficult standards enunciated by Jesus on the shores of the Sea of Galilee?

Gandhi is both emphatic and clear that choices need to be made. He says: 'That you cannot serve God and Mammon is an economic truth of the highest value. We have to make our choice' (Parel, H.S., 2009; CW 1999, v. 15, p. 277). The crux of the argument here is between wealth as being useful in its instrumental cloak, and as being used as an end in itself which merits pursuit. Mammon is the god of wealth. One cannot, and presumably one should not, pursue wealth as if it were a god, which is what the expression 'serving Mammon' would imply. Gandhi goes on to quote from Shakespeare's *Macbeth* to suggest that trying to accomplish service to both is doomed to failure, not just because the Bible says so but because the Bard also concurs. And then, in this inimitable style, the Mahatma pulls a rabbit out of his hat. He starts quoting from an evolutionary biologist, A.R. Wallace, who has his own idiosyncratic views on matters far removed from biology. Wallace is, for instance, not particularly convinced that there has been 'moral progress' through evolution and history. At the personal level, which is always important to the Mahatma, wealth can turn into an albatross that prevents entry into God's realm. Gandhi is not an advocate of grinding holy poverty. That issue has been dealt with summarily and emphatically. His concern now moves to the rich. Here, ironically enough, wealth is not seen as instrumental for a desirable, ethical objective, but as actually instrumental in spiritually debilitating the human being. And the reference to Mammon suggests that Gandhi is one with the Gospels in opposing an idolatry based on wealth. Here are the beginnings of an ethic that will not countenance unrestricted pursuit of GDP growth at a national level, unhindered focus on market capitalization at the level of a business or continuous wealth maximization at an individual level. Worship of the wretched and false idol Mammon must necessarily be rejected.

Even though he may have been speaking to students, and perhaps especially because he was speaking to students, and even though his subject was economics and not politics, it appears as though the Mahatma was determined to put a stake in the ground that no one could ignore. Therefore, he reverts to the central issue of his political career: Is British rule desirable? Unlike other more restricted thinkers, he realizes that he has to deal with broader issues of economic development in order to answer this question. And as the Rudolphs have pointed out (Rudolph and Rudolph, 2010), Gandhi could and did appeal to the 'other West'. In this case, the 'other West' just happened to be an itinerant Palestinian Jew called Jesus. And it was through the image of Jesus that the Mahatma exhorted young Indians not to copy Britain, 'because she provides us with rulers' (Parel, H.S., 2009; CW, 1999, v. 15, p. 278). In the context of colonial and imperial encounters, the polymath philosopher Ashis Nandy has made a strong case that the ruler too emerged as a wounded and traumatized sufferer (Nandy, 2009). Gandhi is suggesting that if Indians took to pursuing wealth in an untrammelled manner as the appropriate way to imitate the British, not only would they jeopardize their own souls, but, guess what, they would not even be following the precepts of the greatest book of the English—their Bible!

The Mahatma, as is usual with him, remains difficult to pin down, simultaneously ambiguous and startlingly clear, and ever contemporary and important. In part, his continued relevance relies on his seemingly effortless and instinctive ability to incorporate the highest of Christian principles in a manner that at first appearance seems simple, but which is actually immersed in complexities, subtleties and enigmatic interrogations that stay with us over time. What can one make of the following: 'Let us seek first the kingdom of God and His righteousness and the irrevocable promise is that everything will be added with us. These are real economics. May you and I treasure them and enforce them in our daily life' (Parel, HS, 2009; CW 1999, v. 15, p. 279). He sounds like a Christian preacher—not a Roman Catholic or a High Church Anglican, but an English non-conformist, in love with the Bible. This leads us almost inexorably to our next topic—the Mahatma and the Quakers.

Gandhi and the Quakers

Gandhi was reasonably eclectic in his friendships with Christians of different persuasions. Shirer had noticed that the Mahatma had a strong attraction to the Gospels and was somewhat wary of the stern God of the Old Testament (Shirer, 1980). While the Rudolphs talk of Gandhi's intellectual relationship with the 'other West', including Thoreau, Ruskin, and Tolstoy (Rudolph and Rudolph, 2010), Ram Guha has written extensively in more than one place of Gandhi's contacts with his own contemporaries of both Jewish and Christian faiths (Guha, 2013; Guha, 2018). The most well known of Gandhi's Christian interlocutors was Charles Andrews, an Anglican who was devoted to pacifism, the cause of Indian freedom and the plight of Indian-origin indentured labour. Arguably, the Gandhi–Andrews relationship was primarily political (Guha, 2018). The same can be said about the Mahatma's engagement with the Indian Jesuit, Father Jerome D'Souza, who was introduced to Gandhi by C. Rajagopalachari. D'Souza went on to distinguish himself as a member of India's Constituent Assembly. But the Quakers (the denomination formally referred to as the Society of Friends) were clearly the Christian group closest to the Mahatma, both intellectually and emotionally. They were early opponents of slavery; they worked hard for prison reforms; they were opposed to extravagant living; they were fierce practitioners of non-violent pacifism; and for our purposes, they were uncomfortable with inherited wealth. Guha makes reference to the connections between various Quakers and Gandhi. Reginald Reynolds stands out for his political views. His classic *White Sahibs in India* (Reynolds, 1937) was a brutal indictment of British rule. S.E. Stokes was an American Quaker who took on an Indian, even a Hindu, incarnation as Satyanand Stokes and ended up being possibly the only American to be arrested by the British government in India for his support to Gandhi and India's freedom movement—a rather unique achievement! Gandhi wrote sarcastically about the British inability to countenance Stokes's views (CW, 1999, v. 25, p. 200). Marjorie Sykes was a Quaker whose involvement with Gandhi and social and educational reform in India was a result of her early interactions with Rajagopalachari (Rengarajan, 2005). Agatha Harrison was born a Methodist. Methodists are another Protestant Christian group. Harrison gave up Methodism and became a Quaker by choice. She hosted Gandhi during his visit to London to attend the Round Table Conference in 1931 (Guha, 2011). By accepting Quaker hospitality, Gandhi was almost anticipating the Rudolphs' argument about his connection with the 'other West'. He was telling imperial Britain that he had friends among 'Friends' whose Englishness was not in question. As mentioned earlier, the official name of the Quakers was Society of Friends. Making his first public speech during that trip in 1931 at the Friends Meeting House in Euston Road in London was not so much about turning the other cheek, but about landing a gentle slap in the face for the diehard British imperial ruling class! Of all of Gandhi's Quaker contacts, the most important was Horace Alexander. The oft-repeated story of how this relationship arose is interesting. Alexander's father-in-law, himself a Quaker, was upset about an anti-British speech made by the poet Rabindranath Tagore (Gregory, 2010). Young Horace was sent to India as a peace-making envoy. He deserves a measure of credit for the dialogue between Gandhi and Viceroy Lord Irwin that resulted in the historic Gandhi-Irwin pact signed on 5 March 1931 (Gregory, 2010). It was the Gandhi–Irwin meeting that drew the ire of the fanatical imperialist Winston Churchill. Again, a point being made that 'friendships' can exist and flourish even as the Churchills of the world ranted against them. Gandhi acknowledged Alexander's contribution to his efforts handsomely when he visited the Quaker settlement at Woodbrooke in October 1931. He said: 'I have come here as a matter of pilgrimage because this Settlement it was that spared and sent Mr Horace Alexander to us at a time when we were in need of a friend' (CW, 1999, v. 54, p. 43). Gandhi was a master of linguistic usage. The pun on the word 'friend' and the choice of the word 'pilgrim', recalling John Bunyan, the great English writer whose famous book *The Pilgrim's Progress* also belonged to the 'other' Christian tradition (not the mainstream Anglican one, supported by the English upper classes), could both not have been accidents. It is important to keep in mind that while Bunyan or the Quakers may be considered 'other' in so far as they were not mainstream Anglicans, they were definitely very English. As for the King James Bible— it is clearly quintessentially English. Reverting to the Quakers, an important footnote is that the wardens of the Woodbrooke centre were Henry and Lucy Cadbury, descendants of John Cadbury, the Quaker businessman who founded the well-known eponymous cocoa and chocolate company. The present writer was pleasantly surprised to find that a Harvard Business School professor, Geoffrey Jones, is researching George Cadbury as an exemplar of an ethical and compassionate businessperson. As a business historian, Jones is interested in a range of Quaker businesspersons and their contribution to a refreshing and innovative approach to the morality of market capitalism: Barclay, Lloyd, Fry, Rowntree, Cadbury, Allen, Hanbury, Clark, and Reckitt are all part of the list of illustrious English Quaker businesspersons who to this day are mentioned with respect because of their commitment to principles and ethics. We will revisit Rowntree and Cadbury presently.

Gandhi's love affair with the Gospels predates his deep engagement with Quakers. One cannot therefore postulate the existence of a Quaker influence on Gandhi's intellectual development with the same clarity and importance one notices in the direct influence of Mark and Matthew. Nevertheless, it is fascinating to take note of the parallels and overlaps between the Mahatma's thought processes and those of the Quakers. Perhaps that is why Gandhi and so many Quakers became so close and in such a public manner. The great early Quaker leader William Penn has written as follows: 'The Godliness does not turn us out of the world, but enables us to live better in it, and excites our endeavors to mend it' (Loukes, 1960). The resemblance of this point of view to what the American historian Barton Scott while writing about Gandhi refers to as 'worldly asceticism' is quite clear (Scott, 2016). Quakers were pacifists and, on many occasions, became conscientious objectors to wars in their personal capacities. Clearly, this resonated with Gandhi's emphasis on non-violence in his political activity. Quaker interest in obtaining justice for India and Indians was not a twentieth-century phenomenon. Harold Loukes in *The Discovery of Quakerism* reminds us that John Bright, an early Quaker member of the British Parliament in the nineteenth century, 'worked also at the problems of India and Ireland, pressing for wider powers and larger liberties for these people whom it was customary then to regard as inferior and untrustworthy' (Loukes, 1960). When it comes to wealth, stewardship and inheritance, it appears as though Gandhi and prominent Quakers share an identical hymn book. Writing in the 1 December 2016 issue of *Friends Journal,* Henry B. Freeman quotes a wealthy Quaker as saying: 'Being good stewards of money is valued among Friends, while impressing people with how much money you have is not' (Freeman, 2016). This could quite easily have been Gandhi speaking to a group of Gujarati or Marwari businessmen, many of whom were his admirers, supporters and bankrollers. Freeman goes on to make the point that 'There is a deeply embedded belief among Friends that we live in a society that places far too much emphasis on money as an end in itself . . . Friends instead embrace the concept that money is a useful tool' (Freeman, 2016). The idea that money and wealth are not ends in themselves but of instrumental value is central to Gandhi, who has the same obsessions that many Quakers had, as to how to ensure a moral and benign use of this instrument (Freeman, 2016; Loukes, 1960). Gandhi freely advised his rich friends not to bequeath too much wealth to their offspring, but to provide their children with good education. Gandhi was concerned about the negative effect of wealth on the children themselves (CW, 1999, v. 82, p. 63). Gandhi felt that easy access to wealth made the children of the rich into lazy and self-indulgent persons. In this, he echoes the Quaker businessman Joseph Pike, who wrote: 'I can say in the sincerity of my heart, that I never inclined or strove to be rich, or to make my children great or high in the world, seeing the ill effects of it in others' (Loukes, 1960).

Benjamin Seebohm Rowntree, son of the wealthy patriarch Joseph Rowntree, in some respects resembled J.C. Kumarappa, the Indian Christian who was a friend and associate of the Mahatma's and who is widely regarded as an outstanding Gandhian economist (Guha, 2018). Kumarappa was concerned about practical solutions to the extreme poverty prevalent in India (Kumarappa, 1951). Seebohm Rowntree resembled Kumarappa in that he was not simply a person who had directionless compassion. He wanted to understand poverty. He published 'Poverty, A Study of Town Life' (Rowntree, 2009) and other research works in the then unfashionable field of the economics of poverty. This made him an authority both on public policy and on private endeavours in that area. Seebohm Rowntree influenced several of the public policies of British Prime Minister Lloyd George. After winning the 1906 general elections, Lloyd George's Liberal Party government introduced social legislation, which involved active government intervention by way of welfare measures. Seebohm Rowntree's well-known empirical methodology around the definition of the poverty line was of great value to Lloyd George's government. The Cadbury family too has kept faith with its Quaker roots and the consequent commitment to ethical, compassionate capitalism. The seminal and extremely significant report on corporate governance, which has influenced so much legislation and impacted many practices in different countries around the world was the handiwork of the Cadbury Committee, presided over by Sir Adrian Cadbury, a worthy descendant of John Cadbury (Cadbury, 1992).

The Gospels influenced Gandhi. The Quakers influenced Gandhi and in turn were influenced by Gandhi. Marjorie Sykes, Satyanand Stokes and Laurie Baker are among the many brilliant Quakers who can also be considered Gandhians (Guha, 2011). It is important to note that Gandhi was not the only Indian to have influenced the Quakers. The Indian philosopher S. Radhakrishnan influenced Cecil Evans, a prominent twentieth-century Quaker scholar. Radhakrishnan was holding a chair at Oxford when Evans was a student there. In 1939, Radhakrishnan edited a book entitled *Mahatma Gandhi: Essays and Reflections* (Radhakrishnan, 2010). It still remains an authoritative book. It is not an accident that the second essay in the book, which follows Radhakrishnan's own, is written by the Quaker Horace Alexander (Radhakrishnan, 2010). Evans and several other Quakers took the lead in forming a Gandhi Foundation in Britain; the Foundation has focused on recognizing efforts on the continued examination of Gandhi's ideas in multiple fields. A worthy tribute to one who was a 'friend' of the 'Friends'! From the perspective of the Gospels, a perspective that Gandhi endorsed, being rich automatically reduced the likelihood of divine grace for the individual concerned. But an attitude of renunciation and service to fellow-humans could mitigate that risk (Parel, 2006). In an essay on Quaker faith and practice published in 1987, Evans has this to say about their role, which is a sort of categorical imperative for Quakers: 'Our role is to remind the rich and privileged including ourselves, of the challenge to surrender privilege' (Evans, 1987). Truly, or if one prefers the vocabulary of the Authorized Version, 'verily' Gandhi was a Friend. No wonder that Quaker stewardship and Gandhian trusteeship emerge as similar responses to the twin economic issues of poverty and wealth.

Gandhi and the Trappist Monks

While Quakers were Protestant Christians, there was a group of Roman Catholic monks who also had important influence on Gandhi. Gandhi became acquainted with Trappist monks when he visited their monastery outside Durban in South Africa in 1895. Gandhi was impressed with their asceticism, their prayers and their silences. But his most important takeaway seems to have been the Trappist commitment to manual labour. Manual physical labour was to become, over time, a central part of the Mahatma's philosophy of life and of education. With Gandhi, one must always expect the unusual. Hermann Kallenbach, Gandhi's Lithuanian Jewish friend and collaborator in South Africa, visited the Trappist monks and learned the craft of shoe-making. Kallenbach introduced Gandhi and his followers to shoe-making. Over the years, this craft became central wherever Gandhi went and was included as part of Gandhi's proposed educational curriculum. So, that is the story of how a Trappist–Jewish lesson plan eventually entered Gandhi's Nai Talim or New Learning programme!

Tridip Suhrud, who was supervising the Sabarmati Ashram in Ahmedabad in 2013 when I spoke to him, drew my attention to the fact that the Cistercian Trappists were similar to the Augustinian order to which the famous geneticist Gregor Mendel belonged. Mendel developed his theories of heredity from empirical data that he acquired from the messy manual activity of gardening. The idea that hands-on practical work is something which actually helps in the development of good theories recurs in the thoughts of J.C. Kumarappa, Gandhi's associate, who wrote extensively on Nai Talim.

5

Gandhi and the Isavasya Upanishad[*]

Gandhi and the Isavasya Upanishad

It is the contention of this book that in order to understand Gandhi's position on political economy, one needs to understand the sources of Gandhi's ideas. Who influenced him? And how? In the religious field, the influences of the Bhagavad Gita, Tulsidas's Ramcharitmanas, Gujarati Vaishnava hymns, and the Sermon on the Mount (Parel, HS, 2009) on Gandhi are well known. In this chapter, I propose to review the influence that the Isavasya Upanishad (also sometimes referred to as the Isa Upanishad) had on Gandhi, and how it accounts for Gandhi's surprisingly unusual and radical views on wealth, capitalism and trusteeship. It is further the contention of this chapter that Gandhi's views on the Isa Upanishad should not be straitjacketed into traditional monist and pluralist interpretations, or even simplistically fitted into modern scholarly perspectives. The Mahatma's own views need to be gleaned not only from what he directly writes and says, but also from the overall approach of his

---

[*] A shortened, summarized variant of this chapter has been converted by me into a standalone article and published in *Swarajya*.

actions. Practicality was never far from his central concerns, and as he remarked, his life and actions were perhaps more important as his message than his words (CW, 1999, v. 23, p. 150).

The Mahatma was not acquainted with Sanskrit. (He did pick up a smattering during one of his long sojourns in a British jail!) We are told that he read not only the Theosophist English translation of the Upanishads, but several other translations too (Parel, HS, 2009).

What is not in question, as mentioned earlier in the opening chapter, is his saying that if all other Hindu scriptures were lost but only the opening verses of the Isa Upanishad preserved, then Hinduism, or at least Hinduism as Gandhi visualized it, would still survive. This is a pretty strong endorsement of the Upanishad, and tells us that while the Gita, the Manas and Vaishnava hymns were undoubtedly important in the development of Gandhi's persona, the Upanishads, and this one in particular, need greater attention on the part of Gandhian scholars. In passing, it may be important to note that since Gandhi derived his knowledge of Indian classical scriptures like the Isa Upanishad from English translations—e.g., Edwin Arnold's translation of the Bhagavad Gita and the Theosophist translation of the Upanishads—there is an orientalist lens to Gandhi's vision. The insights Gandhi claimed to draw from India's classical texts and civilization came through a nineteenth-century European prism (Parel, HS, 2009; Scott, 2016). This is not the place to argue whether such an influence was good or bad. It is the place to take note of the fact that the Mahatma, who is often portrayed as a self-conscious Indian with a pronounced bias against Western civilization, was, for better or worse, an intellectual heir of Western orientalism. Needless to say, it is my contention that this influence was on balance for the better.

The Isavasya Upanishad in the Classical Hindu Context

The Isavasya Upanishad is one of the authoritative texts of the Vedanta school, which is one of the six schools of Hindu philosophical thought that have acquired an aura of orthodox approbation (the other five schools are: Nyaya, Vaiseshika, Sankhya, Yoga and Mimamsa). Traditionally, all the Upanishads—which have been the subject of commentaries by Adi Shankara—are part of the Prasthana-traya, or the three authoritative fountainheads of Vedanta—the other two being the Bhagavad Gita and the Brahmasutras of Veda Vyaasa. The Isavasya, which is a 'poetic' rather than a prose text appended to the Shukla Yajur Veda, is clearly one of the authoritative Upanishads. Following Shankara, the other great Acharyas, Ramanuja and Madhva, have also written commentaries on this Upanishad. These three Acharyas are seen as the founders of Advaita (Monism or non-Dualism), Visishta Advaita (Qualified Monism or qualified non-Dualism), and Dvaita (Dualism or perhaps Pluralism), respectively, these being the points of view from which they interpret the Isa and other Upanishads as well as the two other Prasthana-traya texts. Shankara's later followers, with their emphasis on Mayavada, or the Doctrine of Illusion, can be regarded as extreme Monists (Radhakrishnan, 2006; Deussen, 1966). The Isavasya's opening lines are a good place to contrast these ideas. While the extreme Monists would take the position that the Universe is in fact the Lord, the other schools would take the position that the Universe is pervaded by the Lord or is energized by the Lord. In any event, for all Vedantic schools, the Lord (Brahman, or in the case of this Upanishad, Isa) is central to the Universe. To that extent, the Vedantic schools would differ from non-Vedantic persuasions, which may not attach centrality to the figure of the Lord.

People like the writer and controversial historian Nirad Chaudhuri have argued that Gandhi's inspiration was from medieval Bhakti-oriented popular hymnal literature rather than from venerable Sanskritic sources (Chaudhuri, 1965). Gandhi's attachment to the Isavasya would suggest that this is in fact not the case. In the Isa, Gandhi was seeking inspiration from a text that has stamped on it all the characteristics of great importance and legitimacy going back in antiquity. This too points to the apparent paradoxes in Gandhi's intellectual make-up. Nirad Chaudhuri has argued that Gandhi was not a scholar or even a representative of what he refers to as 'high' Hinduism, but resembled a popular 'bhagat' typically dispensing a 'low' folk Hinduism to his followers (Chaudhuri, 1965). Ironically, those who wish to see Gandhi as a subaltern leader may go along with this view. But, as with so many other things about the Mahatma, just when you think he has been pigeonholed into a box, he breaks free and surprises you with another facet of his persona, pointing to another unexpected source that influenced his complex and variegated mind. Even as Gandhi drew upon the Gujarati vernacular poet Narsi Mehta, whose immortal hymn 'Vaishnava Janato' certainly inspired Gandhi (Parel, 2006), it by no means replaces the influence of the high classical text represented by the Isa Upanishad.

Gandhi was not a classical scholarly *bhasyakaara* or commentator who specialized in verse-by-verse elucidations. Hence, we cannot analyse in detail why exactly he attached so much importance to the Isa Upanishad. But as we explore the Upanishad, especially its opening sequence, we can undertake the journey that the Mahatma made and seek the path that lead to the brilliant outcomes he was capable of. Being an unusually short poetic Upanishad, and one associated directly with a Vedic Samhita, or body of hymns, rather than with supplementary texts like the Aranyakas or Brahmanas, as most of the other Upanishads composed in prose are, the Isa has garnered a lot of interest. There is endless debate as to its exact antiquity, as to whether it is pre-Buddhist or post-Buddhist, and of course as to its proper interpretation, which goes all the way from pretty pure monism to emphatic pluralism (Griffith, 1987; Deussen, 1966; Radhakrishnan, 2006). Curiously enough, the Isa also allows for a bridge between detached asceticism and morally informed material fulfilment. Both are envisioned to be intellectually legitimate.

Starting with a simple working translation of the expression of 'Isa' as having 'the Lord' as its equivalent, it appears that the Upanishad opens with the maxim: the moving universe is enveloped by the Lord. Depending on the strength of one's monistic interpretation, one can argue that the universe is nothing but the manifestation of the Lord—the Lord verily is the universe. More pluralistic views would suggest that the universe is pervaded by the Lord, or interestingly, that the universe is activated or energized by the Lord. Net-net, one is left with an overwhelming impression that the universe exists on account of the Lord, is imbued by the Lord and in fact could be nothing but the Lord itself (note: not himself or herself, as henotheistic interpretations of 'Isa' as a male Lord extend beyond the Upanishad itself and are derived, if needed from priors that the interpreter takes for granted). Of course, extreme monistic approaches could result in the argument that as the Lord and the 'Self' are one and the same, it is one's own Self that envelopes the world and that is in fact the entirety of the universe (Griffith, 1987; Deussen, 1966; Radhakrishnan, 2006). Again, this line of argument really extends beyond the Upanishad itself and is dependent on strongly monistic priors in the mind of the interpreter. Katz and Egenes, who follow Radhakrishnan and Mahesh Yogi, have a pretty convincing translation. It represents a delicate balance between monism and pluralism: 'Everything here, whatever moves in the moving world, is pervaded by the Lord' (Katz and Egenes, 2015). Gandhi's approach was that this world is sacred—a position that is obvious if the Lord pervades this world. Gandhi had no qualms about discussing death. In contrast, he avoided discussing the 'next' world. The sacred nature of this world led almost effortlessly to a requirement that Gandhi himself approach it with a sense of responsibility and realism. He could not and did not treat the world as an illusion, as he remained till his last breath a restless, energetic and determined actor.

The last line of the first verse of the Isa is short and, on the surface, relatively simple. Griffith's academic translation is as follows: 'Covet no wealth of any man.' Swami Krishnananda starts off with a similar version: 'Do not covet anybody's wealth.' But being of the monist persuasion, he adds characteristically, within brackets: 'Do not covet, for whose is wealth?' (Krishnananda, n.d.) In this case, it is not just another man's wealth that is not to be coveted. It is wealth of any kind. And why is wealth of any kind not to be coveted? The answer is quite simple: because it belongs to the Lord. All wealth is the Lord's, as the Lord pervades all. Literally, coveting this is almost inherently meaningless, foolish and trivial in the extreme. Some of Shankara's extreme monist followers go one step further. If the Self and the Lord are one and the same, then how can the Self covet that which already belongs to the Self, that which in fact is the Self? (Griffith, 1987; Deussen, 1966; Radhakrishnan, 2006.) Medieval Hindu monist thinkers had probably not heard of the Greek legend of Narcissus (Graves, 2011). Gandhi, who had written a rather more-than-candid autobiography of his early years, was acutely conscious of the temptations of self-love (Gandhi, 2001). It is unlikely that he would have considered the entire world as his own or as himself. The Madhva pluralistic translation, 'Do not seek anyone else's wealth', is closest to Gandhi's position. This point is important, as I come back to discuss the ultimate trajectory and multiple destinations of Gandhi's thought process.

The middle portion of the opening verse of the Isa is the one that is fraught with the most difficult interpretational challenges, because it straddles asceticism and material fulfilment in the enigmatic, puzzling way so characteristic of all the Upanishads, providing each generation of translators and commentators with plenty of meaningful activity. Katz and Egenes opt for this version: 'Enjoy it (the World) by way of relinquishing it' (Katz and Egenes, 2015). In the opinion of these scholars, the mystery of how one enjoys something by way of relinquishing it would not be something that can be explained or intellectually comprehended. It lies therefore in the realm of experience. When the knowledge that Isa pervades the moving universe is embedded deep within the interstices of the mind, then the revelation as to what constitutes simultaneous renunciation and enjoyment will follow. The Madhva tradition prefers a robust statement: 'Enjoy whatever is given to you by Him.' Note the quiet entry of the henotheistic male Lord. Note also the unabashed invitation to enjoy the Lord's gift. There is almost a Judeo-Christian spirit here, suggesting that the world's gifts are given to humans by the Lord, for enjoyment (Radhakrishnan, 2006). Unsaid, but probably automatically understood by followers, would be that such enjoyment should be in accordance with dharmic principles. Griffith is a little puzzling, but similar. 'With that renounced, enjoy thyself,' is how he puts it. The enigma as to what he implies by 'that' is not explained (Griffith, 1987). What is this mysterious 'that' which is renounced? Swami Krishnananda is more straightforward. He translates as follows: 'Protect yourself through that detachment.' No mention here of enjoying anything. The emphasis is on 'protecting' oneself, again an almost Judeo-Christian concern about temptations and attempts to avoid them (Krishnananda, n.d.). An early twentieth-century English translation of Shankara's version published in Madras has a characteristic directness: 'Through such renunciation do thou save thyself' (Shankara, 1905). If one ploughs through the thousands of pages of Gandhi's *Collected Works* or charts the course of his life and activities, it does not appear that enjoying the gifts of the world, even if such gifts come from the Lord, was high on his priority list. Gandhi, with his obsession for reducing and simplifying his wants, his enforced asceticism, his frequent fasts and penances, would probably have gone along with Katz and Egenes in arguing that the act of renunciation was in fact enjoyable. Or alternatively, he might have preferred the terse Shankara version— that Gandhi could save himself only by way of renunciation. It is not inappropriate to hypothesize that Gandhi would have preferred an eclectic multi-tonal interpretation, leveraging Monism in one place and Pluralism in another. His ability to synthesize different traditions can also be noted in his approach to Christian texts. His two favourite hymns were 'Abide with Me', written by Henry Francis Lyte, a Scottish Protestant, and 'Lead Kindly Light', written by John Henry Newman, an English Catholic (Parel, HS, 2009).

Reconciling Gandhi's Vision with the Classical

So where do all these hair-splitting discussions and our hypotheses of Gandhi's thought processes leave us, apropos of his views on property, wealth, trusteeship, capitalism, socialism and so on? And as the Mahatma himself might have pondered: are there any practical lessons out there? At a minimum, let us establish what Gandhi's version of the famous opening verse of the Isa implies. He would have viewed the world as sacred because the Lord pervaded the world. The existence of the all-pervading Lord can be seen as something that Gandhi took for granted. He would not have opted for enjoying the gifts of the world, but for renouncing them. The idea of protecting himself from temptation would have struck a chord with him. And he would have gone along with not coveting wealth, whether the wealth belonged to others or to the public realm.

If the world is sacred, then humans are at best trustees of the world. They are not, as anthropocentric thinkers might suggest, the rulers of the world. They are temporary inhabitants who need to deal with the external world as a sacred trust, not very different from the fiduciary responsibilities that Gandhi's studies of English law would have suggested to him. This idea of the world pervaded by the Lord being a Trust given to humans, as distinct from a world given to humans to 'lord over', and hence literally act as Lords, is a powerful one, which although not explicitly enunciated by Gandhi, has been taken forward by contemporary environmentalists. Chandi Prasad Bhatt and Sunderlal Bahuguna have acknowledged Gandhi's influence. Indira Gandhi, in her famous Stockholm speech on the environment, quoted not the Isa Upanishad, but the Atharva Veda, and her quotation is in keeping with the thought that the world needs to be treated gently as it does not belong to humans but is pervaded by divinity. The Atharva Veda urges humans not to hit the 'vitals' or 'heart' of Mother Earth (Indira Gandhi, 1975).

Gandhi would practise renunciation, which automatically would have dwelt well with his ascetic tendencies. And, of course, he would not covet wealth of any kind. What does this imply about the economic system that he would have supported? A sacred world is not an illusion. The Mayavada doctrine of extreme Monists would have no place in Gandhi's worldview. The world is a real place where Gandhi and his followers needed to act. The argument for renunciation, from Gandhi's point of view, would be akin to Shankara's. The Lord pervades the world; hence it is to the Lord that the world belongs. In renouncing possession and attempts to own or dominate the world, one only confirms the Lord's pervasive presence, and in the bargain, one saves oneself from conceit, arrogance and hubris. Given his oft-stated dislike for a strong centralized state (CW, 1999, v. 98, p. 314), one thing is clear—Gandhi could not have gone along with at least the socialist doctrine of expropriation of wealth. So, certainly he would have agreed with the proposition of not coveting the wealth of others. I would argue that on the question of individuals not coveting any wealth, Gandhi might have adopted a dual standard. For himself, he would have been perfectly willing to agree that he would not covet any wealth. For others, he is unlikely to have adopted the same position. His friendship with several Indian capitalists and his exhortations to them to act as trustees of their wealth makes sense only in this context. When he set up his Indian headquarters in Ahmedabad, he actually mentioned publicly that one of the reasons he was attracted to Ahmedabad was the existence of wealthy and public-minded benefactors there. An entirely Mahatma-like practical twist to a geographic choice! Gandhi collected money for his political and social movements quite openly. He used to auction his autographs in order to raise money, and many of his public meetings ended with fund-raising activities (CW, 1999, v. 47, p. 350; v. 45, p. 327; v. 89, p. 335; v. 63, p. 10). There is no evidence that he actually exhorted any of his businessman friends not to pursue their business activities. *All of this would lead us to the conclusion that for Gandhi, money was instrumental. Money was part of the world, which, the Isa tells us, is pervaded by the Lord. The instrument of money can therefore even have a sacred aura associated with it. But the instrument would fail its purpose if its pursuit happens without abandoning covetousness, without adopting renunciation, without rejecting the temptations of self-centredness.* But if embraced in the spirit of the Lord whose sacredness pervades it, money could even serve as the means to a constructive engagement with the Lord's universe. Such an engagement would allow for the instrument of wealth to be used to serve broader humanity. Net-net, a convoluted but by no means unconvincing derivation of Gandhi's philosophy, if that is the appropriate expression, from the Isa Upanishad, which in his own words inspired him.

Like many of his contemporaries, Gandhi was strongly influenced by Dadabhai Naoroji's views that Britain had 'drained' India of its wealth (Naoroji, 2010). (Naoroji is cited in *Hind Swaraj* and his work is included in the recommended reading list at the end of the book.) While this may have been a complex economic phenomenon, one must assume that English military law and custom permitted, and perhaps even encouraged, victorious soldiers to collect booty as part of their legitimate compensation (Davis, 1994). The idea of plunder of the vanquished infidel also has legitimacy in Islamic jurisprudence (Kamali, 2002). Clearly, the Isa Upanishad will not stand for this. If even coveting the wealth of another is frowned upon, the actual forcible dispossession of another is completely unacceptable. This can be seen as reinforcing property rights, not just of fellow-citizens, which English law may have approved of, but that of anyone, and therefore, even that of one's adversaries. Gandhi was perfectly willing to negotiate, transact and bargain. But he was at all times opposed to expropriation, and of course to the perverse idea of booty. William Shirer was given a close view of Gandhi's various exercises and excursions during the Round Table Conference in England. This is one of Shirer's reports: 'I will try,' he said, 'to present my position to the cotton-mill workers of Lancashire, hundreds of thousands of whom are out of work due largely to our Indian boycott' (Shirer, 1980). He would tell them, he hinted, that if their government gave India independence the boycott would end and their factories might start humming again.' Reporting on Gandhi's brilliant tour-de-force extempore speech at the Round Table Conference, Shirer has this to say:

> He went on, picturing a glorious future for the two nations, Great Britain and India, working together in equal partnership. I had never heard Gandhi indulge in such flattery, given his dim view of the British . . . 'take these two nations together, and I ask you whether . . . an honorable partnership would not be beneficial, even in terms of your domestic affairs'.

And in keeping with the *Isa's* dictum of not coveting what belongs to others, Gandhi also makes the point that India does not wish to ask Britain to pay off the debt legitimately accrued to India. Shirer quotes Gandhi: "'I say that the Congress never dreamed of repudiating a single claim or burden it should justly discharge. If we are to live as an honourable nation, worthy of commanding credit from the world, we will pay every farthing of our legitimate debt.'" Shirer's own commentary is incandescent in its brilliance. 'Judging by the expression on their faces it seemed evident that the last thing the British authorities in the hall expected to hear from the saintly Mahatma was this excursion into the intricacies of government debt, finance and credit.' And Shirer's own evaluation caps it all: 'What could this amazing Hindu bring up next!' (Shirer, 1980). We need to come back to Shirer's reference to Gandhi, the Hindu, as this is central to our understanding of the sources and eventual directions of the Mahatma's thought processes. But let's continue with Shirer's account of Gandhi's visit to Manchester:

> . . . in a talk with the mill owners, he was more specific. He told them that if India were granted self-rule he would propose ban on the importation of all foreign cloth into India except that from Lancashire. He urged the industrialists to send that message to their representatives in Parliament. 'You see,' Gandhi explained,

like the old trader he could be on such occasions, 'it would just be a case of friendly business relations between two equal partners. We would not like to discriminate against Japan, the United States and western Europe. But naturally two happy partners could not be blamed for making an arrangement to their mutual interests and benefit.' The manufacturers were delighted. They were businessmen and not politicians. This was evident from the remarks of one of them who rose to reply to Gandhi. 'We do not care,' he said, 'about the political aspects of this question as long as business is resumed and Lancashire rescued from being a cotton graveyard. It would mean everything to us and to our workers.' He estimated that if England could supply the cloth and yarn now being imported into India from Japan, China, America and western Europe, it would put half a million English men and women back to work. Gandhi humbly agreed. (Shirer, 1980.)

One could argue that Shirer's extensive reporting truly shows up Gandhi as a person who, while not coveting the wealth of others, was willing and able to enjoy the world as given to him, by way of India's market access, and use this to negotiate and bargain. While this may not accord with the notions of free trade as enunciated by Adam Smith or the other great economist Ricardo, it does accord with the Isa Upanishad's instrumental view of wealth. Shirer may or may not have known of Gandhi's position on Hindu scriptures. But Shirer, by specifically referring to the Hindu in Gandhi, captures a central aspect of the Mahatma's persona and philosophy.

One thing is for certain. Gandhi's trusteeship doctrine was not a clever sleight of hand to help legitimize the wealth and the behaviour of his rich friends. It certainly had roots not only in other wellsprings, but it also derived profoundly from the Isavasya Upanishad, a sacred text for which he had the greatest of regard. There is no woolly-headed impractical appeal to rich people, which is again something Gandhi has been accused of. On the contrary, trusteeship ideas can be derived from one of the oldest and most authoritative texts of the

Hindus. The argument that Gandhi's doctrine was and is impractical is one that can be made against virtually all ideals of a similar nature. The great existentialist philosopher Kierkegaard writes that the early Christian fathers were not foolish in setting up ideals which human beings may find difficult, bordering on the impossible, to attain. Kierkegaard viewed this as deliberate (Kierkegaard, 2014). If ideals were easy, they would not be ideals. As the Gospels say, 'Strait is the gate and narrow the path to life.' Or as the English poet Browning put it: 'Ah but a man's reach should exceed his grasp, Or what's a heaven for' ('Andrea del Sarto', Browning, 1994). Gandhi would have strongly argued that the arguments of Kierkegaard and the poetry of Browning additionally justified his insistence that the Isavasya should be a scripture of choice as we go about determining our relationship with our sacred world and as we go about dealing with thorny issues like renunciation and covetousness or their absence.

In practical terms, could Gandhi's insight provide a moral basis for a human society which goes beyond the anthropocentric, which recognizes a real world, but one which is imbued by the presence of the Lord and which calls upon humans to avoid covetousness and follow a path of informed renunciation, which is adopted with the clear-eyed understanding that in doing so the Self saves itself? This is easily the most important question in the realm of political economy that Gandhi challenges us with. Because the answer to such a question is not easy; it does not mean that attempts cannot or should not be made. That would be the Mahatma's almost playful, but deadly serious response.

Gandhi's Quilon and Kottayam Speeches

Luckily for us, although by no means learned commentaries or bhashya, there are two speeches of Gandhi's at Quilon, Haripad and Kottayam in the southern Indian state of Travancore in 1936, which covered Gandhi's views on the Isavasya, which he refers to as the 'Ishopanishad'. The summaries of these speeches were reproduced

in the 30 January 1937 edition of *Harijan,* a journal that Gandhi
started and edited (CW, 1999, v. 70, p. 366–368). It is obvious that
both for politically convenient reasons and on account of his personal
development, Gandhi in the late thirties spends time talking to a
general Indian audience (not elite economics students) about Hindu
scriptures, not the King James Bible. The Mahatma's transparent
honesty does not mean that he does not focus on practicality and
common sense. He first tells his audience that he first read the
Upanishad 'years ago with translation and commentary'. He goes on
to add that he 'learnt it by heart in Yeravda jail', in passing indicating
that British imperial jails had a bit of a school about them! It is at
Quilon that he made his sweeping statement, which I quote in its
entirety: 'I have now come to the final conclusion that if all the
Upanishads and all the other scriptures happened all of a sudden to
be reduced to ashes, and if only the first verse in the Ishopanishad
were left intact in the memory of Hindus, Hinduism would live for
ever.' The transliteration of the Sanskrit verse in Roman script is as
follows:

*Isa-vasyam idam sarvam, yat kincha jagatyaam jagat, tena tyaktena
bunjeeta ma gridhah, kasya svid dhanam.*

The Mahatma goes on to give 'his' translation: 'All this that we see
in this great universe is pervaded by God. Renounce it and enjoy it.'
Gandhi provides an alternative rendering also: 'Enjoy what He gives
you. Do not covet anybody's wealth or possession.' He goes on to
argue that the rest of the Upanishad is merely a commentary on the
first verse and that even the entire Bhagavad Gita is a commentary on
this verse. As always, the Mahatma has a sharp eye and a sharper ear
for seemingly unrelated connections. He says of the verse: 'It seems
to me to satisfy the cravings of the socialist and the communist,
of the philosopher and the economist' (CW, 1999, v. 70, p. 299).
It is beside the point that socialists and communists who may be
busy denying the existence of Gandhi's God will deny his claim.

Gandhi jumps quickly from one point to another. 'God pervades everything'; 'it behooves you to renounce everything and lay it at His feet'; 'the act of renunciation of everything is not a mere physical renunciation but represents a second or new birth' (CW, 1999, v. 70, p. 299). As we go with Gandhi past each milestone, one can almost visualize a grantor taking his wealth aside and setting it up as a trust, and the trustee accepting control over the wealth not as his, but as belonging to the beneficiary of the trust. The legal has been bound to the religious. And Gandhi sees this as the solution to the larger problem of humans living within the human community. He says: '. . . the mantra closes with this magnificent thought: Do not covet anybody's possession. The moment you carry out these precepts you become a wise citizen of the world, living at peace with all lives. It satisfies one's highest aspirations on this earth and hereafter.' And in what someone like the British philosopher Roger Scruton (Scruton, 2014) would appreciate, Gandhi ticks off the atheist doubter: 'No doubt it will not satisfy the aspiration of him who does not believe in God and His undisputed sovereignty.' The Mahatma reaches his own epiphany as he makes the emphatic point that the opening verse of the Upanishad:

> . . . is calculated to satisfy the highest cravings of every human being.
>
> Since He pervades every fibre of my being and of all of you, I derive from it the doctrine of equality of all creatures on earth and it should satisfy the cravings of all philosophical communists . . . my life and that of all who believe in this *mantra* has to be a life of perfect dedication, it follows that it will have to be a life of continual service of our fellow creatures.' (CW, 1999, v. 70, p. 313, 328).

It simply does not matter that philosophical communists, whoever they are, might have different views and that other commentators have not seen the so-called service ethic so emphatically embedded in this Upanishad. The Mahatma makes the connection and the ecstatic leap back to his central concern of how to simultaneously renounce and be of this world. This burning issue, which Parel points out, remains a constant and obsessive concern for Gandhi (Parel, HS, 2009; Parel, 2016). One could argue that while the Upanishad influenced Gandhi, Gandhi moved the interpretation of the Upanishad in his own chosen direction, pretty much in the spirit of all the great scholarly Hindu commentators of antiquity.

6

Gandhi and the Bhagavad Gita

Gandhi and the Bhagavad Gita

Although it is the contention of this book that the understanding of Hindu religious influences on Gandhi's views in the realm of political economy is best done in the context of his engagement with the Isavasya Upanishad, the importance of the Bhagavad Gita in his life cannot be denied, if for no other reason than that Gandhi himself attached great importance to the Gita. Therefore, a chapter needs to be devoted to this subject, even if only a short one. We have now reached the thirties. By now Mahatma Gandhi is established as the undisputed leader of the Indian national movement. Even the British viceroy and his bosses in London have more or less conceded this. The world press has acknowledged this. *Time* magazine, in distant America, put him on its cover in January 1931. And this is when we come across Gandhi's definitive take on the Bhagavad Gita. The 24 August 1934 edition of the *Harijan* carried extracts from a speech that the Mahatma made at Banaras (now Varanasi) to the students of Kashi Vishvavidyalaya University (CW, 1999, v. 64, p. 253–257). (As an aside, in the 'English' atmosphere of Muir College, twenty years earlier, the attention is on the Bible. In the

'Indian' ambience of the Kashi Vishvavidyalaya, the focus is on the Gita.) In that speech, he referred to the Gita as his 'mother'. Gandhi, like many other educated Hindus of the nineteenth and early twentieth century who were influenced by the West, was looking for the answer to the question: 'Which is the one book that can be to the Hindus what the Bible is to the Christians or the Koran to the Mussalmans?' (CW, 1999, v. 64, p. 254). Ashis Nandy refers to this as 'an attempt to introduce the concept of The Book following the Semitic creeds'. Nandy has noted that the urge to create a central book was widely prevalent among many Hindu intellectuals in the nineteenth and early twentieth centuries. In his classic book *The Intimate Enemy*, Nandy actually refers to this as 'Christianization of Hinduism'. Gandhi is in the company of the nineteenth-century mystic and reformer Swami Vivekananda, whose preferred 'book' was also the Gita, and of the great Bengali writer Bankimchandra, whose imagined 'historicized' prophet of Hinduism was Krishna, the divine interlocutor in the Gita (Nandy, 2009). While it is a perfectly legitimate argument to make that the Indians exposed to Western intellectual traditions found solace and even an element of pride in emphasizing the Gita in their encounter with Christian missionaries who looked down on the heterogeneous, amorphous and non-authoritative nature of so-called Hindu scriptures, it must be noted that the Gita, as well as the Isavasya Upanishad, are traditional classical, canonical texts for Vedantic schools of Hinduism and gain their authority from the fact that the great Adi Shankaracharya and subsequent great acharyas wrote commentaries on both, starting from 700 CE through 1200 CE, long before the so-called British encounter. The Gita is very much a part of the Prasthana-traya or the 'canonical three' that all Vedantic scholars, starting with Adi Shankara and down to Radhakrishnan in the twentieth century, have acknowledged.

Realism in a very basic sense demanded that if Gandhi wanted to be the leader of Indians, the majority of them Hindus, he would have to show an engagement with the Gita. This was a political compulsion, if nothing else. But like everything else about the Mahatma, his approach was always unique and carried his personal stamp of authenticity. It is extremely significant that he refers to the Gita as his 'mother', at one stroke moving away from the masculine approaches to Hinduism that both Bankim Chandra and Vivekananda were votaries of (Nandy, 2009; Nandy 2013). Gandhi has this to say of the Gita: 'When I am in difficulty or distress, I seek refuge in Her bosom' (CW, 1999, v. 64, p. 255). The soft, maternal visioning of the Gita was particularly necessary for Gandhi as he was hard-pressed to stick to his position that the Gita preached non-violence, when in fact the text begins and ends with Krishna exhorting his companion Arjuna to wage a just war. Gandhi's introduction to his Gujarati translation of the Gita, written in 1929, was then translated into English and published in *Young India*'s 6 August 1931 issue. In textbook style, Gandhi makes a series of points. Point no. 8 shows Gandhi's dexterous intelligence, nimble thinking and extraordinary capacity for capacious argumentation, all of which extend rather than constrict inherited traditions. He says:

> Even in 1888-89, when I first became acquainted with the *Gita*, I felt that it was not a historical work, but that, under the guise of physical warfare, it described the duel that perpetually went on in the hearts of mankind, and that physical warfare was brought in merely to make the description of the internal duel more alluring. This preliminary intuition became more confirmed on a closer study of religion and the *Gita*. (CW, 1999 v. 46, p. 167.)

At one stroke the Mahatma adopted the dictum of Humpty Dumpty from *Through the Looking-Glass*. The Gita, or for that matter any other text, was going to mean whatever it was that lawyer Gandhi wanted it to mean. This, of course, gave him the option of converting a manual that is read by many others as an exhortation to war, into a scriptural guide to non-violence. I have often used a technique similar to Gandhi's. When asked whether the Gita encourages or discourages war, my neo-Gandhian response is to plead that I am interested only in economics and not in military affairs!

Gandhi, the Gita and Homo Economicus

As our interest is not in Gandhi's political strategies and tactics, we need not concern ourselves too much as to whether Gandhi's convoluted reading of the Gita is fair or not. We are interested in how the Gita impacted Gandhi's positions in the more limited realm of political economy. As Parel has so elegantly pointed out, Gandhi rejected the excessive asceticism of what Parel refers to as India's '*shramanic* traditions' (Parel, HS, 2009). A monk who retires to a monastery or a yogi who retires to a Himalayan cave are not Gandhi's ideal humans. To him, it was important to stay involved in political activity and service to humanity in this world. This, of course, automatically implied pursuit of economic activity. How is this economic activity to be performed and, more importantly, constrained by ethical boundaries—just the way non-violence was to constrain political acts like civil disobedience? Point no. 14 of his introduction has only one sentence: '*That matchless remedy is renunciation of fruits of action*' (CW, 1999, v. 46, p. 169). Here Gandhi is a classic Hindu traditionalist. Gandhi's translation of arguably the Gita's most famous verse (the verse starting with '*Karmanyeva Adhikaraste*' is the only verse that many people know and quote!), which deals with karmayoga or the 'discipline of action' appears in his point no. 22: 'Do your allotted work but renounce its fruit . . . be detached and work . . . have no desire for reward and work' (CW, 1999, v. 46, p. 172). All the great commentators of the Gita have focused on this extraordinary concept. Human beings have the 'right to work', the 'right to perform their duty', and the 'right to act'. They do not automatically obtain therefore the right to the fruits or rewards of the work/duty/action. This creates a problem for homo economicus, or the so-called 'economic human' right away. If I do not get the fruits and rewards of my work, why would I work at all? Gandhi gets around this simply by asserting that certainly action and work, if not duty, are simply inescapable facts of human life. Again, in point no. 22, he asserts: '. . . all living beings have to do some work, whether they will or no. Here all activity, whether mental or physical, is to be included in the term action' (CW, 1999, v. 46, p. 141). Does this then lead to a trap of laziness, shoddy work and an extreme position of ignoring all consequentialism? As always, Gandhi's practical business sense quickly creeps back in the very next paragraph: 'But renunciation of fruit in no way means indifference to result' (CW, 1999, v. 46, p. 172). With surgical precision, Gandhi demolishes all convenient arguments that can justify laziness, shoddy performance at work, or a casual attitude to labour. In point no. 23, he goes one step further, pretty much openly defending the biblical idea that a workman is worthy of his hire. He says: '. . . let no one consider renunciation to mean want of fruit for the renouncer' (CW, 1999, v. 46, p. 172). What then is this peculiar renunciation all about? Gandhi is simple and emphatic: 'Renunciation means absence of hankering after fruit' (CW, 1999, v. 46, p. 172). I would argue that the choice of the word 'hankering' is not accidental. On one level it ties back to the Isavasya Upanishad's mode of renunciation. It ties in neatly with not being covetous of wealth, especially that of others. Elaborating in point no. 23, the Mahatma becomes a very practical psychologist even as he develops his moral theme: 'He who is ever brooding over the result often loses nerve in the performance of his duty. He becomes impatient and then gives vent to anger and begins to do unworthy things; he jumps from action to action, never remaining faithful to any' (CW, 1999, v. 46, p. 172). It is almost as if Gandhi is describing a business executive who is not interested in good customer service or a quality product, but who is obsessed only with the share price of his firm. And, of course, as night follows day, such obsessions with a perverted set of ends must necessarily result in moral corrosion. Gandhi says: '. . . he is ever distracted, he says goodbye to all scruples, everything is right in his estimation and he therefore resorts to means fair and foul to attain his end' (CW, 1999, v. 46, p. 172). It reads as if it were an indictment of a manipulative businessperson made by a prosecuting attorney. The obvious conclusion is that a trustee who views wealth as pervaded by God and as being instrumental, rather than an end, will not indulge in 'hankering' or 'brooding over'. One could argue that here is an opportunity to pursue an entirely different but related set of arguments on the psychological implications of wealth for the wealthy, and perhaps Gandhi offers a way out of a psychological ailment. Trusteeship constitutes for Gandhi a way out of Arjuna's trap. A trustee pursues the fulfilment of the obligations of his role. Given the trustee's purely fiduciary role, he or she passes on the benefits of the action to others and does not gain directly. A rather neat solution to a recurring human conundrum!

The Idea of the Worldly Ascetic

The historian J. Barton Scott has pointed out the underappreciated fact that the ideas of the great German sociologist Max Weber and those of Gandhi overlap in content and timing. And we cannot forget that Weber was the scholar and implied defender of Western market capitalism (Weber, 2006). Any similarities, therefore, are very useful to buttress our search for Gandhi as an interpreter of market capitalism. Gandhi first read the Bhagavad Gita in its English translation in 1889. This translator was Sir Edwin Arnold, and he referred to the Gita as 'The Song Celestial', which was the title of his translation too (Scott, 2016). Over the next twenty years, Gandhi developed his ideas, which culminated in *Hind Swaraj* in 1909. Max Weber's *The Protestant Ethic and the Spirit of Capitalism* 'took shape between 1904 and 1920' (Scott, 2016). Barton Scott points out:

> . . . in The Song Celestial, Edwin Arnold translated key passages pertaining to karmayoga into an English idiom that strongly evokes Weber's concept of the Protestant work ethic . . . Here, the discipline of action centers on the command to 'do thine allotted

task' because 'work is more excellent than idleness' and Krishna instructs Arjuna to 'live in action! Labour! Make thine acts/Thine piety, casting all self aside'.

Gandhi's early encounter with *The Song Celestial* thus suggests the proximity of his project to the cultural field Weber had set out to analyse. Gandhi in effect follows through on the provocation only implied by Arnold's text: '. . . how could one use the Gita to imagine a Hindu worldly asceticism' (Arnold, 2017; Scott, 2016). Weber's conceptualization of the Protestant ethic and Gandhi's take on the Gita both suggest the imperative of what can be called 'worldly asceticism'—pointing to a convergence of Protestant Christianity and Gandhi's personal Hindu doctrine of the Gita, arrived at through the convoluted lens of Arnold, the Victorian Englishman.

Weber's sober Protestant capitalist pursued material this-worldly activity not for its fruits, but 'solely for the greater glory of God' (Scott, 2016). For good Protestant businesspersons, the religious and the economic were inexorably intertwined. And yet there remains a recurring common anxiety that perhaps this is not the case. Gandhi does not indulge in any deft maneuvre. He deals with the issue head-on. In point no. 24 of his introduction, he says:

> The common belief is that religion is always opposed to material good. "One cannot act religiously in mercantile and such other matters. There is no place for religion in such pursuits; religion is only for attainment of salvation", we hear many worldly-wise people say. In my opinion the author of the Gita has dispelled this delusion. He has drawn no line of demarcation between salvation and worldly pursuits. On the contrary he has shown that religion must rule even our worldly pursuits. (CW, 1999, v. 46, p. 172.)

The choice of the word 'mercantile' is so fitting for Gandhi. He was himself a descendant of merchants and a friend of merchants. The British imperial stereotype of the sly, oily Hindu Bania merchant or the nineteenth-century anti-Semitic European stereotype of the cunning Jewish peddler had no place in Gandhi's world view. He respected his merchant friends and refused to demean or patronize these 'worldly ascetics' by expecting from them a lower or more contaminated ethic than from other-worldly, religious ascetics. The icing on the cake is the Mahatma's assertion of the equal and symmetric necessity of the reverse proposition—the imperative placed on religion itself to remain practically relevant. In the same point no. 24, he says: 'I have felt that the *Gita* teaches us that what cannot be followed out in day-to-day practice cannot be called religion' (CW, 1999, v. 46, p. 172–173). It should be noted that Gandhi could very well have said: 'what cannot be *easily* followed out in day-to-day practice'. But he did not. Nowhere does the Mahatma suggest that following the Gita's message—either as expounded by traditionalists, or as transmuted by Edwin Arnold, or as personally, and perhaps idiosyncratically, elucidated by Gandhi himself—was or can ever be an easy task. But the Mahatma never shied away from the obligations of performing a task merely because it was difficult. The Gita ends by stating that 'victory' is inevitable where Krishna and Arjuna are found together. Gandhi's point that there is no 'indifference' to result and that there is 'no want of fruit' by the act of renunciation seems to be elegantly echoed. For the Mahatma, this victory would have been embedded in the moral compass of the action itself in 'this world' and not in any other. And the Gita being his mother, this moral compass is inevitably imbued not with any machismo but with maternal compassion.

7

Adam Smith and the Mahatma[*]

The Many Facets of Gandhi and Smith

Books written for students of economics and management make no references to Mahatma Gandhi. The losers are the students. Gandhi, with his encyclopedic range of interests, has much to say that can be treated as complementary to mainstream economics and management theories, or as even an intrinsic part of them. His contributions, even at their most eccentric, have a universal appeal, as Ramachandra Guha (2018) points out, and are characterized not only by high idealism, which one undoubtedly expects from a great soul, but also by their almost invariably empirical grounding and suitability for wide practical application. Attempting to make an intellectual connection between Gandhi and Adam Smith, the 'father' of economics, may appear to be a formidable task, given that Gandhi is popularly associated with asceticism and anti-industrialism. But I would submit that this task is no more formidable than the philosopher Akeel Bilgrami's attempt to

---

[*] A shortened, summarized variant of this chapter has been converted into a standalone paper jointly authored by Shishir Jha and myself.

establish linkages between Gandhi and Marx. Bilgrami makes the case that many of Gandhi's criticisms of modern civilization 'had to do with the wrongs in particular of the social, cultural, and cognitive fall-out of capitalist economies'. The atheist Marx and the intensely religious Gandhi in this case are ideologically connected in their common approach to the 'fallout' of capitalism. Looked at this way, Bilgrami's approach does not appear to be contrived or convoluted. Bilgrami goes on to make the case that both Gandhi's and Marx's approaches to norms and values are at the opposite ends of that of David Hume and Adam Smith, the quintessential philosophers of the Scottish Enlightenment and possibly the 'original' philosophers of market capitalism (Bilgrami, 2012; Bilgrami, 2015). It is not my intent here to explore Bilgrami's brilliant exposition. My point of departure is that irrespective of the ex-ante priors, the net result of the approaches of Gandhi and Adam Smith can in fact end up having an uncanny congruence.

I submit that my approach in seeking parallels between the agnostic Adam Smith and the religious or spiritual Gandhi is not particularly convoluted or unrealistic. For this, one needs to go back to the Adam Smith of the *Theory of Moral Sentiments*, published some seventeen years before the *Wealth of Nations*. This outstanding work of Smith on moral philosophy can be seen as the precursor and as the foundation without which his treatise on political economy would not have a proper context (Smith, 2002). I am grateful to Professor Amartya Sen for directing me to Smith's earlier work in order to fully understand a philosopher who had much more to say than the oft-quoted sentence from the *Wealth of Nations*: 'It is not from the benevolence of the butcher, the brewer or the baker that we expect our dinner, but from their regard to their own interest' (Smith, 1982). The younger Smith of the *Theory of Moral Sentiments* suggests that each of us derives a personal moral compass by referring to 'an impartial spectator' who exists as a 'man within the breast' (Smith, 2002). The 'impartial spectator' presumably stands close to but outside a human being and watches the actions and behaviours of that person. The analogous nature of Gandhi's 'still small voice within' (CW, 1999, v. 76, p. 349) of his conscience is not to be missed. It is interesting to note that while making reference to the voice of conscience, Gandhi does not seek to directly bring in God or religion. In fact, as early as in January 1907, while in South Africa, Gandhi adopted a completely humanist vision when he wrote in *Indian Opinion*: 'Man has two windows to his mind: through one he can see his own self as it is; through the other, he can see what it ought to be.' (CW, 1999, v. 6, p. 214), Writing about Smith's position, his biographer Nicholas Phillipson makes the point that 'Sometimes the voice of the impartial spectator would be judgemental, and sound like the voice of conscience or even of the deity himself' (Phillipson, 2010). The believer Gandhi skips the deity, whom the agnostic Smith invokes—admittedly indirectly. A neat juxtaposition that has a trace of irony about it! Nowhere is the symmetry between Smith's theory regarding the moral imperatives that drive human beings and Gandhi's position seen better than in the supremacy that they assign to the 'impartial spectator' and to one's 'conscience'. Gandhi has this to say: 'There is a higher court than the courts of justice and that is the court of conscience.' Phillipson argues that for Smith the impartial spectator 'had come to mean more', 'than the judgement of friends and acquaintances' (Phillipson, 2010). Despite the supreme position assigned to the impartial spectator and to one's conscience by Smith and by Gandhi, respectively, the interesting thing is that both were acutely sensitive to the need to attempt one's level best to extend one's personal moral judgements into the sphere of social interactions with other human beings. One could argue that independent of each other, the Scotsman who admired commerce and the Gujarati Bania who was a child of commerce, intuitively felt the need to make morality and social discourse compatible. Smith talks about the need to 'humble the arrogance of self-love, and bring it down to something which other men can go along with'. The German scholar Dieter Rothermund sums up the similar position of Gandhi's, where he wanted to humble himself in order to 'convince his adversary' (Rothermund, 1992). The spiritual Gandhi, who spent a lifetime wrestling with his conscience and seeking his God, and the agnostic Smith, who is careful never to give a religious patina to his impartial spectator, nevertheless end up not only with a moral vision that has similarities, but also with a similar concern for practical social consequences, as seen in their concern for 'something which other men can go along with'—or, in Gandhi's case, with 'convincing adversaries' like the British rulers.

The attempt to establish an intellectual linkage between Smith and Gandhi should not be seen as trying to force a square peg into a round hole. It stems from an estimation of Smith as a sensitive moral philosopher, whose capacious mind travelled well beyond economic formulations. Simultaneously, Gandhi needs to be seen beyond his caricature as an ascetic, anti-industrial Luddite. We need to keep in mind that Gandhi said and wrote a great deal over the years, not all of which can be comfortably placed in a single convenient philosophical box. Smith has been too often identified with economists of the utilitarian school who followed him and may have derived their ideas based on their interpretations of Smith. The utilitarian school, associated with the two British thinkers Jeremy Bentham and John Stuart Mill, is known for its popular maxim, 'the greatest good of the greatest number'. Gandhi was concerned with the poorest person in the society and the simplistic additive formula of aggregation did not meet with his approval. There is almost an analogous parallel when Amartya Sen emphatically points out that the association of Smith with the utilitarian school does not make Smith a simple-minded utilitarian. Gandhi's support of free markets should not surprise anyone who is acquainted with Gandhi's emphasis on individual freedom, his distrust of a behemoth state and his lifelong association with traders and businessmen, first as clients in South Africa and later as friends, patrons and political associates, both in South Africa and in India. It must be noted that Gandhi had ample opportunity to change his position over the years, especially given the fact that his political associates Nehru and Bose were votaries of socialism.

The irrepressible and unpredictable Mahatma did in fact try to take the wind out of the sails of his detractors by proclaiming that he too was a socialist. The fact that he did not believe in class struggle or the expropriation of wealth resulted in the socialist intellectuals dismissing Gandhi as a hypocrite, a challenge which he simply glided past with the elegance and humour that was characteristic of him. Smith's position as a moral philosopher precedes his acquisition of the title of 'father of economics'. Analysing Smith and Gandhi jointly is by no means a strained exercise.

The Empiricist Gandhi

One of the most compelling summaries of the universal nature of Gandhi's influence and the wide range of his impact comes from the British historian Judith Brown, who has this to say:

> Gandhi was no plaster saint. Nor did he find lasting and real solutions to many of the problems he encountered. Possibly he did not see the implications of some of them. He was a man of his time and place, with a particular philosophical and religious background, facing a specific political and social situation. He was also deeply human, capable of heights and depths of sensation and vision, of great enlightenment and dire doubt, and the roots of his attitudes and actions were deep and tangled, as are most people's. He made good and bad choices. He hurt some, yet consoled and sustained many. He was caught in compromises inevitable in public life. But fundamentally he was a man of vision and action, who asked many of the profoundest questions that face humankind as it struggles to live in community. It was this confrontation out of a real humanity which marks his true stature and which makes his struggles and glimpses of truth of enduring significance. As a man of his time who asked the deepest questions, even though he could not answer them, he became a man for all times and all places (Brown, 1991).

It is important to remember that in addition to being a historian, Brown is an ordained Christian priest. Hence her ability to incisively take note of the wrestling and churning within Gandhi's mind and soul as he sought the right combination of the religious and the practical. Carrying this argument forward is the brilliant Iranian-Canadian philosopher Ramin Jahanbegloo, who has this to say: 'We need to stop holding Gandhi captive to his common public image in order that he might help us to break free toward our most creative and dialogical future' (Jahanbegloo, 2013). Gandhi's thoughts on the duties of a trustee did not arise in a vacuum. They were built on the solid foundation of his insights that rights and duties are two sides of the same coin. He has this to say on the subject: 'If we all discharge our duties, rights will not be far to seek. If, leaving duties unperformed we run after rights, they will escape us like a will-o'-the wisp' (CW, 1999, v. 30, p. 68). It is almost as if an English barrister were holding forth to say that in a thoughtful and well-thought-out contract, rights arise when the contracting party has performed his or her part of the contract. It is important to keep coming back to Brown's elegant words: '. . . questions that face humankind as it struggles to live in community' (Brown, 1991). Jahanbegloo captures the significance of the challenge of living in community when he has this to say: 'One of Gandhi's primary concerns was thus to explain how an individual self as a moral agent in a political realm always stands in relation to other human beings' (Jahanbegloo, 2013). Needless to say, living in community and being a moral agent relating to other human beings are the very core interests that inspired Adam Smith's long intellectual life.

The Rudolphs have argued with some justification that Gandhi's political economy ideas were influenced by the 'other West' (Rudolph and Rudolph, 2010). Gandhi in their opinion was part of a dissident and often underestimated tradition with Western thought. They make a case for Gandhi being a post-modernist, or at least a pioneer of what would today be identified as post-modernism, which presumably questions several fundamental assumptions of the more traditional intellectual currents of Western philosophy. While this argument has its attractions, the case can also be made that Gandhi was not that far removed from these traditions, as we will presently see. The scholar Naresh Dadhich has cogently analysed Gandhi's critique of modernity, which traditionally has been compared with the thought processes of John Ruskin and Leo Tolstoy and made the case for seeing parallels in it with the French philosopher Rousseau (Dadhich, 2008). In the light of these weighty intellectual arguments and Gandhi's oft-quoted sarcastic comment that 'modern civilization would be a good idea' (Bakshi, 2012), it seems difficult to establish parallels with the strong empirical and non-didactic elements that constitute Adam Smith's Scottish enlightenment positions. Forcing such a fit seems neither tenable nor desirable. And yet, the parallels do hold and there remain sufficient arguments in Gandhi's own words and in the responses of noted Gandhian scholars to help us make this seemingly difficult journey. The Gandhian intellectual scholar Joseph Prabhu makes the key point that the so-called religious Gandhi was very much a practical empiricist. To quote Prabhu: 'Gandhi is fundamentally concerned with practice rather than with theory or abstract thought, and such philosophy as he used was meant to reveal the "truth" in the crucible of experience' (Prabhu, 2008). This would take us almost effortlessly into the world of David Hume and Adam Smith as that pretty much represents so much of their world view. Prabhu further argues that Gandhi's choice of words in a very important situation was no accident. 'Hence the subtitle of his autobiography—"the story of my experiments with truth". The experiments refer to the fact that the truth of concepts, values and ideals is fulfilled only in practice' (Prabhu, 2008).

Perhaps the person who shows the sources of Gandhi's robust empiricism best is the scholar Anthony Parel, who ascribes the development of Gandhi's ideas, or for that matter his ideals, not to the oft-mentioned 'other West', but to somewhere deep in the interstices of traditional Hindu thought. Roderick Matthews writes a panegyric to Parel: '. . . perhaps the best recent interpretation of

Gandhi as thinker and politician comes from Professor Anthony Parel, who edited and prefaced a contemporary reprint of *Hind Swaraj* in 2009. Anyone who wishes to read a brief and lucid interpretation of Gandhi's political thought should seek out this slim volume' (Matthews, 2012). It is interesting that Parel has gone back to the *Hind Swaraj*, which was frequently politely and patronizingly dismissed by modernists and modernizers like Nehru (Parel, HS, 2009). The Mahatma himself maintained on more than one occasion that *Hind Swaraj* was his original and ongoing testament and that he was not at all inclined to change the positions and words he had first articulated in it as early as in 1909 (Parel, HS, 2009; CW, 1999, v. 15, p. 156). Parel deserves credit for the strong and emphatic assertion that we need to go beyond the cleverness which most of us see in Gandhi's oft-quoted comment that modern civilization would be a 'good idea'. Gandhi's intent was to warn India and the world about the seductive nature of what superficially passes for modernity. Gandhi was concerned that any civilization, be it early Indian civilization or the emerging universal civilization, needed to concern itself with the 'object of life'. Parel takes this up as concern with 'the canonical aims of life', or the 'purusharthas' as articulated by classical Hindu thinkers. The four traditional purusharthas or pursuits that man (or more appropriately, human beings—more about Gandhi's gender views later) needs to be dealing with are: dharma (virtue and ethical integrity), artha (wealth and political power), kama (passion and pleasure), and moksha (spiritual transcendence). Parel makes the point that Gandhi was quite clear that apropos of his commentary on Indian civilization and Indian philosophical traditions, Gandhi was an 'innovator' who 'has a surprise for us'. The new civilization that India needs has to be mediated by the modern type of political and economic institutions and practices, and by Western values such as rights, civil liberty, gender equality, economic development, rule of law, civic nationalism, etc. It would also need a major aesthetic facelift of India, affecting its public health, hygiene, sanitation, the arts, architecture and village and urban renewal . . . His concern for aesthetics—should anyone doubt it—is the reason why he asks the readers of *Hind Swaraj* to read Tolstoy's *What is Art* and Ruskin's *Political Economy of Art*.

From Parel's perspective, Gandhi is someone who is acutely aware of the limitations of contemporary India circa 1909. 'What is defective in current Indian civilization is its overemphasis on other-worldliness and asceticism (on moksha) and an under-emphasis on this worldliness and engagement with the world (artha). What Indian civilization needs is realignment of the 'canonical aims of life', and an end to the predominance of the ascetic tradition over culture' (Parel, 2006; Parel, HS, 2009; Parel, 2016). Right there is a brilliant riposte to the usual arguments, bolstered by numerous Gandhi quotations that one can safely dig up from all over his *Collected Works,* which would suggest that all that Gandhi stood for and posited was an ascetic, spiritual, village, pre-industrial Indian civilization as an antithesis to the ways of the West—an approach which so irritated modernists like George Orwell, who at the end of the day found himself forced to disagree with Gandhi and even mildly dislike him. We need to substantively debunk Gandhi's ascetic reputation, based on his under-emphasis of what Parel refers to as '*shramanic* traditions' (which can be loosely interpreted as ascetic traditions) in dealing with the purusharthas (Parel, HS, 2009). Only then can we fully explain Gandhi's variegated philosophy.

Moralist Smith and Economist Gandhi

Almost symmetrically, one needs to make sure that we don't exaggerate the importance of simplistic utilitarian fundamentalists who may have been inspired by Adam Smith, but who cannot be taken to be the only interpreters, followers or intellectual descendants of Smith. In recent times, Amartya Sen has done a yeoman service in terms of freeing Smith from his reductionist followers—both extreme utilitarians and extreme neo-classicists who seem to have made pareto-optimality into a religious principle. Sen has ably argued that Smith's quotation about 'the butcher, the brewer or the baker' refers to the limited area of the economics of exchange (Sen, 2010). To emphasize this quotation and to exclude the enormous range of material that Smith has left behind in his capacity as a moral philosopher, is to really do a great disservice to the sage of the Scottish Enlightenment. Similarly, the economic principle of pareto-optimality is simply descriptive of a state where one party cannot gain any more in an exchange without a loss to another party. It has no normative or ethical connotations whatsoever, and to describe such a state that at one level may be economically efficient and therefore as morally desirable, is completely uncalled for. An extraordinary line in Smith's *Theory of Moral Sentiments* is worth recalling: '. . . the chief part of human happiness arises from the consciousness of being beloved' (Smith, 2002). If there indeed exists a craving for being loved inside each of us, then it would be out of place to think of ourselves simply as utility-maximizing economic units. Nicholas Phillipson pertinently points out that Smith maintained as follows: '. . . the moral sensibility of the ethically sensitive person had been shaped by some other agency than the opinions of others' (Phillipson, 2010). In other words, one may want to be loved. This, however, does not automatically result in saying or doing things merely in order to be loved. Paradoxically and marvellously, it entails listening to the 'impartial spectator', the 'man within the breast' (Smith, 2002). It is not surprising that while reviewing *Theory of Moral Sentiments*, the English conservative philosopher Edmund Burke had this to say: 'Philosophers therefore very frequently miss a thousand things that might be of infinite advantage, though the rude Swain treads daily on them with his clouted Shoon (shoes). It seems to require that infantine simplicity which despises nothing, to make a good Philosopher as well as to make a good Christian' (Phillipson, 2010). Gandhi would have approved of the unobtrusive introduction of the religious angle by Burke by referring to what makes a 'good Christian', even if this was far from the intent of the agnostic Smith. Gandhi would have also approved of the superiority of the rude Swain's ('swain' is an old English word for 'peasant') understanding over that of the fancy philosopher! Among Gandhi's disciples, people like Nehru objected to what they saw as a regressive outlook on the Mahatma's part, which resulted for instance in his disliking machinery and idealizing villages (Parel, HS, 2009). But in reading and re-reading the philosophers of the past (and Gandhi's *Hind Swaraj*, now more than a century old, belongs to the past), if one does not apply nuance and take a proper contextual view, then one is apt to get locked into simplistic binaries. Consider this quotation from David Hume, the great Scottish philosopher who was Adam Smith's good friend: 'Another advantage of industry and of refinements in the mechanical arts, is, that they commonly produce some refinements in the liberal: nor can one be carried to perfection, without being accompanied, in some degree, with the other' (Hume, 2012). Place alongside this quotation something that the Mahatma once said: 'Take the case of the Singer Sewing Machine. It is one of the few useful things ever invented, and there is a romance about the device itself. Singer saw his wife labouring over the tedious process of sewing and seaming with her own hands, and simply out of his love for her he devised the sewing machine, in order to save her from unnecessary labour' (CW, 1999, v. 29, p. 266). Whether the Mahatma's charming story about the notoriously polygamist, philandering Singer's marital life (Jones and Kiron, 2017) is true or not, it makes for a very memorable way to communicate the instrumental nature of Gandhi's approach to industrial transformations. Gandhi's own inner voice judges the goodness of an invention, provided the inner voice decrees that there is a contribution to human happiness. If nothing else, Gandhi's admiration for the Singer sewing machine goes to prove that he was not entirely against industrialization. Adam Smith would have understood and related to the same instrumental approach, as he argued in *Wealth of Nations,* that the principle that guides mankind is one of 'bettering our condition' (Smith, 1982), something that the inventor Singer had almost certainly done.

Two Anti-Imperialists

It is easy to dismiss evidence of congruence between the agnostic Scottish economist and the religious Gujarati Bania politician as merely digging up isolated quotations out of context and trying to force-fit analogies and similarities. One area where this argument can be made quite easily and quite appropriately is in the approach that both Smith and Gandhi had towards the baneful effects of colonialism and the pitfalls of aggressive nationalism. Smith, along with his English friend Edmund Burke, was a lifelong opponent of the East India Company. He rightly surmised that the monopoly position of the company resulted in benefits of Indian trade accruing not to all Britons, but to the select few who were the company's shareholders. Additionally, Phillipson points out that for Smith '. . . it was not acceptable to allow these monopolies to become all but permanent in a way that ensured that the civil and military government of vast territories like India were subordinated to the interests of a single commercial organization' (Phillipson, 2010). Writing Additions and Corrections to his *Wealth of Nations* in its third edition in 1784, Smith says: 'It seems impossible . . . to render these courts, in any respect, fit to govern, or even share in the government of a great empire; because the greater part of their members must always have too little interest in the prosperity of that empire, to give any serious attention to what may promote it.' (Smith, 1982).

According to Phillipson, what Smith envisaged was an end of the East India Company, or at least its monopoly, which he felt would probably lead it to wither away. Smith also envisaged an end to a commercial organization being a ruler. And this would result in 'as great a revolution in Britain's relations with the orient as the loss of the American colonies had brought about in the West, a revolution which would usher in a new liberal global order' (Phillipson, 2010). Burke, with his proposals for Parliamentary commissioners to supervise the newly acquired Indian territories, while respecting the traditions of the people therein, was also pushing for what can loosely be called the conservative alternative, but which by historical standards would have been a radical one indeed (Mukherjee, 2005; O'Brien, 2015).

If Smith and Burke had prevailed, the Indo-British encounter may have resulted in greater economic prosperity for India rather than its impoverishment, and ironically greater prosperity for all classes of Britons, not just that of a small and powerful mercantile group. Smith and Burke ended up as two friends who emerged as Cassandras who were not believed. Over the next century and some, British trade with tiny Argentina amounted to more than trade with India as the low purchasing power of Indians made them improbable customers. Two authors who are cited in *Hind Swaraj* are Dadabhai Naoroji (Naoroji, 2010) and Romesh Chandra Dutt (Dutt, 2013), who echoed Smith in their writings on the Indian economy. Gandhi had an intuitive grasp of the potential for increasing Indo-British trade for the mutual benefit of the two countries at the Round Table Conference, as has been mentioned earlier. He actually proposed to Lancashire industrialists that in the event of early independence, India could and would consider preferential tariff in Lancashire's favour (Shirer, 1980).

Gandhi was not opposed to beneficial trade between India and Britain. Virtually every page of *Hind Swaraj* drips with his intense dislike for top-down imposed trading infirmities that were resulting in India losing at the global trade table, and the fact that these infirmities existed because of colonial rule (Parel, HS, 2009). Gandhi found it particularly appalling in the context of Queen Victoria's proclamation that attempted to take the high moral ground of the Crown operating for the benefit of all subjects. Gandhi would have approved of Smith's statement: 'To hurt in any degree the interest of any order of citizens, for no other purpose but to promote that of some other, is evidently contrary to that justice and equality of treatment which the sovereign owes to all the different orders of subjects' (Phillipson, 2010).

Smith was very conscious of the dangerous consequences of regulatory capture by powerful vested interests. Regulatory capture refers to the situation where rich and powerful interests literally control the government and force the government to implement policies, not for the general good of citizens, but for the good of these limited sectional interests. Gandhi went one step further as he took to task not just the principal beneficiaries of imperial regulatory capture, the British mercantile interests, but also their Indian accomplices who presumably picked up the proverbial crumbs. The idea that regulatory capture can result in several sets of beneficiaries, some who can be seen as the primary and others as secondary beneficiaries, constitutes an interesting economic insight in and of itself. Numerous secondary beneficiaries may be crucial to allowing an equilibrium situation to develop in favour of the principal beneficiaries. It is not accidental that Gandhi's *Hind Swaraj* is addressed primarily to the Indians who are collaborators, beneficiaries and supporters of the 'British system'. If such support is withdrawn, then Gandhi argues, in political terms, that the Raj would almost certainly collapse. While this has extensive ramifications in the literature of political movements of dissent (Jahanbegloo, 2013; Brown, 1991), the fallout in the realm of purely economic thought is deserving of a separate analysis. This subject repeatedly crops up in *Hind Swaraj* (Parel, HS, 2009) and deserves an in-depth examination as we go on to consider the eventual directions of Gandhi's views on political economy and the development of his doctrine of trusteeship.

Smith and Gandhi independently saw the dangers of aggressive nationalism and the baneful effects it could have on the well-being and prosperity of people. Gandhi quotes the Boer leader Kruger, who said that it was highly unlikely that there was gold in the moon, because if there were, then the English would have annexed the moon (CW, 1999, v. 10, p. 263). Phillipson refers to the 'difficult ethical question for the modern citizen in deciding how much he owed his country. An uncritical love of country could all too easily lead him to view "with the most malignant jealousy and envy, the prosperity and aggrandizement of any neighbouring nation" and was a form of false patriotism that he (Smith) and Hume had always regarded as a potentially fatal threat to the security, prosperity and public finances of Britain and France' (Phillipson, 2010). Smith wrote thus about the two super-powers of his day: 'France and England may each have some reason to dread the increase of the naval and military power of the other, but for either of them to envy the internal happiness and prosperity of the other . . . is surely beneath the dignity of two such great nations' (Phillipson, 2010). Here we see Smith, the moral philosopher par excellence. The American journalist Louis Fischer has made the point that the Mahatma was concerned that the doctrine of 'an eye for an eye would leave the world blind' (Fischer, 2015). So, here we have two different moral philosophers coming from distinct traditions, by no means identical in their visions, but worthy participants in a dialogue that we, their heirs, can benefit from.

8

Gandhi and the Purusharthas

Yuga Dharma and Purusharthas

There is a tradition in Indian philosophical scholarship where a 'commentator', while holding forth on an earlier text, tradition or thinker, can innovate by way of expansion, abridgment or change of emphasis. This implies not a complete rejection of a previously respected or revered position, but definitely an altered or fresh perspective. Historians like A.L. Basham (Basham, 2004) and philosophers like Radhakrishnan (Radhakrishnan, 2006) have commented on this typically Indic manner of building on tradition, not jettisoning it, but many a time so radically altering it that in effect a break occurs in tradition, even as at a formal level the tradition is reaffirmed. Especially apropos of ethical thought, this approach can claim considerable antiquity. The Indian concept of '*yuga dharma*' or 'morality as appropriate to a particular time/age/epoch' is actually derived from positions enunciated in ancient texts like the *Apastamba Sutra*, attached to the *Yajur Veda*. The Indologist PV Kane dates this text to circa 450 BCE (Kane, 1958). The concept of yuga dharma was central to Gandhi's approach. While asserting the importance of eternal verities, he was nevertheless acutely conscious of the fact the morality needs to be reinterpreted for each age. Global imperialism was the central historical fact of the year 1909. The moral arguments of *Hind Swaraj* (Parel, HS, 2009) commanded attention because they were relevant to that age. The argument can be made that the *Hind Swaraj* outlines the yuga dharma appropriate for a conquered people—Indians in the age of global imperialism.

Without explicitly positioning himself as an authoritative '*bhashyakara*' or commentator, the Mahatma nevertheless played this role with respect to the doctrine of purusharthas. This doctrine, while alluded to in Vedic sutras dated to the first millennium BCE, is subsequently extensively discussed in the epics, the Ramayana and the Mahabharata, and in the Tamil classic, the *Tirukkural*. The compound word 'purushartha' can be split into 'purusha' (man or human or cosmic being) and 'artha' (goal, aim, objective, or end). Gandhi, being a practical empiricist, was acquainted with the fact that as the word 'purusha' had passed from ancient to modern Sanskrit and to other languages, it had lost the possibility of luminous translations like 'the citadel of dawn' and had become in common parlance 'man', with a clear masculine gender bias, as Parel points out (Parel, HS, 2009). Gandhi would have none of this. It was important for him to establish the universal nature of 'purusha'. He conducts his own etymological journey as follows: 'That which dwells in the *pura*, the body, is *purusha*. If we interpret the word purushartha in this sense, it can be used equally for men and women' (CW, 1999, v. 49, p. 437). Naïve, so-called radical anti-Gandhians should note the fact that Gandhi, at least here, emerges as a sober and emphatic feminist.

The four canonical purusharthas are kama, artha, dharma and moksha. Kama can be variously interpreted as passion, or as the pleasure principle or as an Indian correlate of the Greek eros. Indians have always been aware that when distorted, kama can descend into dysfunctional sensuality and lust. On the other hand, when elevated and a tad exalted, kama can be transformed into a refined aesthetic sensibility that connects with the *nava-rasas* or nine essences that help create and define an artistic endeavour. Artha can be interpreted simply as material wealth or as political power—the classical Indian text on statecraft is called the *Arthashastra* or the Science of Artha (Basham, 2004). Although there is no evidence of Gandhi using the expression 'political economy', it turns out that it would have been ideal to describe his explorations of artha. Dharma is a capacious word that pervades all Indian languages in one form or the other. The writer Gurcharan Das has described it as the central motif of Indian civilization (Das, 2010). It has been interpreted as virtue, righteousness, duty, obligations enjoined upon a person on account of his or her position in life, stage of life and situation as reflected by the caste he or she is born into. The classical writers were quite clear that the imperatives of dharma have an overarching importance. The pursuit of either kama or artha without its being informed by and influenced by dharma was behaviour that needed to be shunned by noble persons. This was the critical foundation on which Gandhi built his entire approach to political economy.

Dharma as righteousness or right conduct was central to Gandhi in worldly matters; hence the Gandhian scholar Nishikant Kolge makes the case that in political and economic matters, apropos of caste and gender, Gandhi played the role of a typical commentator in the Indian tradition. Kolge says Gandhi did not jettison or overthrow inherited positions; in fact, at least in part and on the surface, he appeared to agree with them. But both through words and deeds Gandhi acted in a manner that radically reinterpreted the underlying concept (of dharma) in a manner that a new yuga dharma is the result (Kolge, 2017). Gandhi did not explicitly jettison caste. But the end result of his intellectual and practical wanderings is a version of caste that is so fundamentally different from the way he first found it, that it might very well be described as something entirely different, but still referred to as caste. The point that Kolge has developed brilliantly in his book is of great importance if we have to deal with the criticism that Gandhi's insights, being tainted by his support for the traditional caste system, are of little value in engaging with the modern world. In fact, it is Gandhi's modernity, if that is the right expression, which leads to his becoming the subversive Indic commentator on caste and indeed on gender issues (Kolge, 2017).

When it comes to moksha or salvation or liberation, or seeing 'God face to face' as Gandhi put it, he was in complete agreement with the traditionalists that this purushartha was clearly the most important one that transcended the others and in fact could and should be viewed as the end of the other three. Gandhi did not reinterpret moksha in the manner he did dharma. He simply questioned the excessive asceticism that had seeped into the quest for moksha. Parel refers to this as Gandhi's disagreement with the *shramanic* world view (Parel, HS, 2009) which, while being a part of the earliest Indic traditions, was nevertheless subject to periodic reassessments in terms of emphasis. For Gandhi, the way to attain moksha involved immersion in the pursuit of artha, which he interpreted as action in the political sphere (Parel, HS, 2009). It is this shift of emphasis—away from asceticism and the search for individual moksha and towards active involvement in this world and pursuit of worldly goals—that characterizes Gandhi's approach to the purushartha doctrine. The 'ashrams' or retreats of moksha-seeking ascetics were deep inside forests or in Himalayan caves. Gandhi used the term 'ashram' to describe the living and working spaces of his associates and himself.

The Kochrab and Sabarmati ashrams were situated in thriving cities, and the Sevagram ashram was situated bang in the centre of India—no hint of abandoning this world and retreating into lonely ascetic austerities here. The dichotomy between Gandhi's choice of the word 'ashram' and the way these ashrams operated in practice is not a trivial one and goes beyond the matter of their location. In a traditional Indian ashram, the inmates are older persons, usually single and usually those who have 'abandoned' the world in order to seek salvation. The contrasts with Gandhi's ashrams are striking. The inmates of Gandhi's ashrams belonged to all ages. While communal prayers were part of the routine at

Gandhi's ashrams, the inmates were required to do much more than just practise meditation, contemplation, breathing exercises or prayers. They were required to spend time in manual labour: gardening, spinning, leatherwork, carpentry and so on. The inmates included whole families. Children were an integral part of the ashrams, and their educational needs were addressed. Gandhi's ashrams were very much part of this world and not retreats that pursued asceticism. In fact, their subliminal message seems to have been to tell people to focus on active involvement in economic and political matters. The Indian ashrams of Gandhi followed from his earlier experiments in South Africa, where these establishments were referred to as the Phoenix Settlement and the Tolstoy Farm—the names indicating active work. In fact, in most of his ashrams, Gandhi ran a printing press and emphasized economic activity to raise resources to support the ashrams, at least in part. Willy-nilly, Gandhi moved the canonical pursuits of the purusharthas in the direction of artha—but artha informed by dharma—economic and political pursuits which had of necessity to be informed by virtue and righteousness. Even as he built on antique traditions, Gandhi moved towards a radical moral position.

The Imperatives of Yuga Dharma

Parel makes the point that Gandhi was emphatic that in the times he lived in, non-involvement in political matters was not an option (Parel, HS, 2009). Therein lies an important facet of the Mahatma's unique approach. He embraced Western ideals. Roman law was one of his favourite subjects in his London days and influenced him considerably (CW, 1999, v. 44, p. 152). The imperative of involvement in civic affairs in one's role as a citizen, in Roman terms, and as a human (purusha), in Gandhi's version of Indic terminology, is typical of Gandhi's ability to effortlessly meld thoughts and maxims on his own terms. Like Humpty Dumpty in *Through the Looking-Glass*, Gandhi seems to have forever been intent on being the master of his words and his message. The role of the concerned and informed citizen occurs as a repetitive motif in Gandhi's words and actions. Even as he fought with a mighty empire as part of his political travails, Gandhi remained endlessly and intensively involved in issues of sanitation, civic order and so on. He also subtly undermined the caste system even as he kept making equivocal statements about it. Kolge makes the point that unlike other Hindu revivalists, Gandhi never 'asked' of his Dalit and lower-caste followers that they imitate upper-caste practices, which presumably were more refined. On the contrary, he insisted that his family members and ashram compatriots regularly clean toilets, usually considered a polluting task meant only for outcastes.

Even more interestingly, one of the tasks that Gandhi favoured was leatherwork, particularly shoe-making. This too was considered a highly polluting activity by Hindu traditionalists and was forbidden for the upper castes. This inversion in action in terms of caste is very typical of Gandhi's ethical messages. He was conveying messages about the dignity of labour—something dear to his heart—subtly sabotaging the caste system while ostensibly not opposing it. It was the Mahatma's duty, his dharma, if you will in the times he lived in, in his yuga if you will, to reaffirm the importance of worldly activity by setting up his ashrams in cities and literally in the middle of the country, and by staying focused on an astonishing range of civic issues. He also restores pride in all honest labour by turning the issues of pollution and cleanliness on their head. In pursuing artha informed by dharma in this manner, Gandhi renders considerations of moksha irrelevant on one level and virtually an inexorable fallout at another level. In this approach, again he is in good company as far as Indic intellectual traditions go. The scholar P.S. Sundaram has pointed out that the Tamil classic, the *Tirukkural*, which might date back to the second century BCE, is focused on '*muppaal*' or the three divisions of kama, artha and dharma. The omission of the fourth purushartha is ostensibly because 'the proper pursuit of the other three will inevitably lead' to moksha. Sundaram goes on to note that the Shanti-Parva of the Mahabharata also chooses to discuss only the three divisions known as '*trivargas*' (Sundaram, 1990).

Parel draws our attention to the fact that Gandhi attached tremendous importance to service (Parel, HS, 2009). Yuga dharma demanded that the purusha serve the world and its inhabitants. As in virtually all his messages, Gandhi starts with the intensely personal and radiates outwards to the wider world. He would personally nurse sick people. And, of course, he recruited, organized and supervised an ambulance brigade of stretcher-bearers and nurses during the Zulu War (CW, 1999, v. 21, p. 105). Starting with the personal and then moving on to active involvement in the world is the crucial requirement of yuga dharma, which will not be satisfied with the pursuit of individual salvation in isolation. When it comes to the economic aspects of artha, Gandhi is quite clear that entrepreneurs create wealth, and depriving entrepreneurs of their wealth would end up harming society at large (CW, 1999, v. 40, p. 102). We are unlikely to find a more apposite defence of the free enterprise system among other political leaders of his time. But excess wealth, transmission of excess wealth by way of inheritance, and illegitimate instrumental use of wealth—all of this is fraught with a-dharmic dangers. And it is here that the strategic insights of the Mahabharata and the *Tirukkural* come to the rescue. In the absence of balance between the purusharthas, a human pilgrim gets trapped in quicksand. A balanced pursuit of artha and dharma is Gandhi's persistent message. Support for entrepreneurial freedom does not lead to support for the love of money. He quotes from the Gospels in his speech to the students at Allahabad in 1916, when he reminds them: '. . . that you cannot serve God and Mammon is an economic truth of the highest volume' (CW, 1999, v. 15, p. 277). Embedded in this insight is perhaps the finest set of normative prescriptions Gandhi can provide to those who are actively engaged in material matters like business and government in this yuga/age.

Gandhi fought for the political independence of his people. This tends to suggest that he was a fighter for their rights. He was certainly such a fighter and was willing to indulge in civil disobedience against unjust laws that violated the rights of his countrymen and countrywomen. But what this analysis misses is that Gandhi was far more obsessed with duties than with rights. The moralist in him insisted that people could not and should not demand rights without in turn fulfilling their obligations. In fact, he has an audacious position—that if people gave sufficient attention to their duties, the rights would follow (CW, 1999, v. 9, p. 459). In the free enterprise system, one could argue that if businesses and entrepreneurs were conscious of their duties, society would automatically confer on them the right to do business and even grant them the halo of special legitimacy. There certainly would be no incentive for society to be hostile towards businesses, let alone to expropriate or nationalize them! The irony in the situation is typical of so much that is associated with Gandhi. Here is an idealist position that can actually result in practical positive consequences.

Independence and Freedom

If *Hind Swaraj* remains the central, seminal text that we need to go back to in order to understand Gandhi, then it makes sense to invest some time and effort in looking at the roots of the word 'swaraj' itself. Swaraj can be translated as 'freedom' or 'independence'. A more chaste translation of the Sanskrit word would actually lead to the expression 'self-rule'. Gandhi constantly emphasized the importance of self-rule at the individual level. In his emphasis on the individual as the all-important unit of society, Gandhi appears as a champion of Western enlightenment principles, although one could argue that it is no more than giving centrality to the traditional Indic purusha. Irrespective of the origins of Gandhi's love of the individual and individuality, the fact is that emphasis on individualism automatically rules out authoritarian, totalitarian and even collectivist approaches to political economy. No wonder Gandhi looks down both on Mussolini and the Bolsheviks (CW, 1999, v. 54, p. 266; v. 43,

p. 127). But we cannot forget that buried in the notion of self-rule is the rejection of hedonism. The contemporary English philosopher Roger Scruton would argue that individual freedom without an inner self-discipline and sensitivity for the sacred will lead one down a catastrophic path (Scruton, 2014). Gandhi would have agreed. Another frequent variation of swaraj has been 'su-raj' which can be translated as 'the rule of the good' or 'the rule of good principles'.

If India became politically free but Indians turned into a fundamentally immoral and a-dharmic people, the 'freedom' struggle would have ended in defeat for them. Without the leavening of dharma, which starts with the individual and goes outward in concentric circles, political freedom is inherently meaningless. Gandhi makes use of the metaphor of concentric circles to describe his ideal polity, in part in order to reject the top-down hierarchical metaphor of the imperial state. But each civic circle that expands, starting from the individual, needs to be touched with the grace of dharmic morality. A large part of *Hind Swaraj* consists of arguments against the violent tactics involved in the nationalist struggle as propounded by contemporary proponents of 'revolutionary' ideas. To inject violence into India's freedom struggle would, in Gandhi's opinion, fatally taint the struggle itself and result in baneful consequences. He was also acutely aware that in practical consequential terms, a violent struggle would in all probability fail and backfire (Parel, HS, 2009). There is no element of hypocrisy in Gandhi's moral position, which is independently arrived at, and in his simultaneous understanding that the position may have good consequences. In fact, he would probably say in his inimitable impish manner, that while the appropriate dharma has to be followed for its own sake, how can one doubt that its consequences will not be beneficial?

Gandhi had various Tamil compatriots in South Africa. His friend and associate in India C. Rajagopalachari published his English translation of parts of the *Tirukkural* well after Gandhi's death. So it is unclear if Gandhi had direct knowledge of the Tamil text, although a certain level of acquaintance is almost certain. To this day the *Tirukkural*, or the *Kural*, as it is sometimes called, remains a foundational text for anyone studying the purushartha philosophies. It is appropriate to conclude this chapter with quotations from the *Kural*, which Gandhi either knew, or would have approved of wholeheartedly, or has himself articulated in different words. The pursuit of artha is important if for no other reason than that contemporary India's 'grinding pauperism' filled Gandhi with horror and that artha was the path away from poverty. Pursue wealth creation or elimination of poverty through the path of *porul*/artha, says the Kural, for, 'There is nothing like poverty but poverty'; such pursuit needs to be done with practical sagacity, for 'It is not wisdom to lose the capital for the sake of interest'. It also needs to be pursued within the battleground bounded by *aram*/dharma, for 'Wealth acquired sinless and well yields both virtue and happiness.' But having pursued porul/artha successfully, one must never forget that it is instrumental for its larger moral purpose, because 'Compassion, child of love, is nourished by wealth, the generous foster-mother' (Sundaram, 1990). Clearly, wealth enables one to become a generous foster-mother—or, in Gandhi's words, a fine trustee!

The argument needs to be pursued to explicate what kind of functioning economic model the Mahatma would have desired and approved of. It would definitely be a 'this-worldly' model, not one which worships poverty, but which has active disdain for 'grinding pauperism' (CW, 1999, v. 15, p. 274). It would view private ownership of wealth and a non-rapacious state as central. It would closely tie ownership of wealth to its simultaneous twinning with moral imperatives. It would view the individual's pursuit of the eternal verities leading to salvation as being automatically achieved if economic pursuits (artha) are intertwined with ethical concerns (dharma). In the absence of such intertwining, the human lot would be fundamentally unsound and not worthy of attention. But if artha and dharma are conjoined, then a desirable and practical economic system will develop, and this system will be beneficial to individuals and the community.

9

Gandhi and Identity Economics

The Contemporary Discipline of Identity Economics

With the publication of 'Economics and Identity' in the *Quarterly Journal of Economics* in 2000, followed up by the book *Identity Economics* in 2010, a new way of thinking about homo economicus (the economic human) emerged (Akerlof and Kranton, 2000; Akerlof and Kranton, 2010). In the introduction to their book, the authors Akerlof and Kranton took pains to set their thought processes and insights within the framework of economics scholarship. As they point out, 'Modern economics follows Adam Smith's attempt in the eighteenth century to turn moral philosophy into a social science designed to create a good society. Smith enlisted all human passions and social institutions in this effort' (Akerlof and Kranton, 2010). They go on to add: 'Fairly recently, behavioural economics has introduced cognitive bias and other psychological findings. Identity economics, in its turn, brings in social context—with a new economic man and woman who resemble real people in real situations' (Akerlof and Kranton, 2010). Identity economics can be described as that branch of behavioural economics which suggests that human beings make economic decisions not only on the basis of monetary incentives, but also as responses to their identity needs. In other words, identity economics postulates that a person's sense of self or identity affects economic outcomes. Interestingly enough, Gandhi would have approved of any study focused on the 'creation of a good society'; he would have wholeheartedly supported engagement with 'human passions and social institutions'. He would have demurred a bit about 'real people in real situations'. While not disagreeing with the need to have firm foundations in the real world, the world of ideals never remains far from the Mahatma, and he would be falling back on St Matthew and St Mark to egg us on towards, at a minimum, aspiring for the ideals posited by Christ, the 'greatest economist of his time' (Parel, HS, 2009; CW 1999, v. 15, p. 275).

Traditional economics views individuals as being selfishly concerned with their own individual 'utilities'. Rather than oppose utilitarianism in a head-on manner, Akerlof and Kranton simply get around simplistic positions by arguing that issues of 'identity and norm' are embedded in the utility functions that economic agents purportedly have. They note: '. . . individuals' behaviour depends on who people think they are' (Akerlof and Kranton, 2010). The parallel that this idea has with Gandhi's thinking is telling. The Mahatma argued repeatedly that the behaviour of rich persons could and would change if they thought of themselves not as owners of wealth, but as trustees of wealth (CW, 1999, v. 50, p. 21). Identity and norms are inextricably tied together. According to the political scientist Jon Elster, norms are the 'cement of society' (Akerlof and Kranton, 2010).

Gandhi was concerned about how the cement held together the members of his various ashrams, who had to adhere to explicitly stated norms (CW, 1999, v. 15, p. 165–175). On a wider scale, he was concerned about the norms needed to cement fellow-Indians, be they Hindus, Muslims, or Untouchables together (Sheean, 2005). When discussing Gandhi's role as an inspiration for modern environmentalists, Ramachandra Guha focuses on Gandhi's emphasis on the negative impact of unbridled consumption (Guha, 2018).

I would argue that the doctrine of trusteeship has an equal if not more important contribution to make in arguments dealing with the natural environment. One of the issues that keep cropping up when we talk about the economics of environmentalism relates to the difficulty of protecting a natural resource (a forest or a river or a lake) which belongs to no one. This is known as the tragedy of the commons. Gandhi's answer would be that dharma or the pursuit of virtue will show a way out. The Nobel laureate Elinor Ostrom makes a similar case when she argues that 'norms' embraced by communities can many times ensure that the tragedy of the commons does not occur. 'Norms', as adopted not only by individuals but as collectively subscribed to by groups of individuals, like the inmates of Gandhi's ashrams, would have been welcomed by Gandhi. The oft-quoted free-rider problem, when one individual or a small group of individuals tries to escape the costs borne by the community as a whole, is in fact solved, because they do not want their identity as good citizens and fair members of their communities to be assailed (Akerlof and Kranton, 2010). Gandhi's trusteeship doctrine could provide an impetus to inter-temporal environmental guidelines, which are guidelines needed when we talk of protecting resources over long periods of time, sometimes even after the deaths of the individuals involved. The behaviour of a trustee of a river, a lake or a well is different from the behaviour of an owner of the same natural resource. After all, these resources at one stroke transcend the ownership construct and are seen as being held in trust for future generations. In Gandhi's native Gujarat, there has been a long tradition of wealthy people building stepwells as endowments for the welfare of future generations. Gandhi would doubtless have been aware of this custom.

In recent times, identity has become an overworked word. The discourse in contemporary media tends to be about religion, ethnicity and sexual orientation. It is important to remember that identity spans much more than these items of current controversy. Writing in 1961, the social psychologist Erving Goffman pointed out that age was a significant determinant of identity. Thirteen-year-old children were ambivalent about enjoying rides on the merry-go-round, because they felt that the norms demanded that younger children should primarily use merry-go-round carousels (Akerlof and Kranton, 2010). The unique thing about identity is that it is not deterministic. While it is true that a short person cannot become a tall person, it does not follow that a short person must define her identity only in terms of absolute or relative height. Amartya Sen makes this case when dealing with contemporary pressures on individuals to define themselves in terms of primordial ethnic or religious identities. A person can be a vegetarian, a Beatles buff, a Chelsea fan, in addition to being a white British Anglican or a brown Hindu Bengali (Sen, 2007). Even the norms of aspiration and desired projection of identity, not just as to how one describes oneself but also as to how one would like to be perceived by others, are not frozen inheritances, but matters where human agency can and does have an impact. This was the approach to identity behind James Coleman's questionnaire addressed to schoolboys, where he asked them the following: 'If you could be remembered here at school for one of the three things below, which one would you want to be: brilliant student, athletic star, or most popular?' (Akerlof and Kranton, 2010). Clearly, norms guide people's self-definitions and definitions of how they would like to be perceived. Akerlof and Kranton have brilliantly analysed the role of gender in identity and how this can have practical impacts on labour markets. 'Women are supposed to stay at home and raise children. They are therefore supposed to move in and out of the labour force, whereas men are not' (Akerlof and Kranton, 2010). Akerlof and Kranton have in those two sentences summarized the prevailing misogynist assumptions that lead to lower wages for women.

How Gandhi Grappled with Identity Issues

It turns out that both in his personal and public life, Gandhi had a unique challenge, which in his own way he converted into an opportunity to grapple with identity issues. Parel points out that Gandhi was trying to lead his countrymen and countrywomen in their capacity as Indians (Parel, HS, 2009). But the objects of the Mahatma's attention stubbornly insisted on identifying themselves by religion—Hindu or Muslim—and by caste—Brahmin, Bania, Dalit, etc. In fact, Gandhi had no choice but to confront a very ancient ethnic and occupational identity, uniquely Indian in its contours—caste. Guha has made the case that simplistic criticisms of Gandhi for not taking an early stance against the caste system completely fail to understand the prevalent zeitgeist among the majority of Hindus when Gandhi started his political career in India (Guha, 2018).

The historian Rajmohan Gandhi too pays attention to the texture of Gandhi's evolving positions on caste (Gandhi, 2017). Nishikant Kolge has done the best analysis of Gandhi's approach to caste identity (Kolge, 2017). It is quite clear that Gandhi chose to attack caste with great intelligence and sensitivity. Caste was by any definition, first and foremost, an identity marker. Deeply embedded in the idea of caste is the idea that certain activities and occupations are considered ritually and practically of a polluting nature. Dealing with human excreta and cleaning toilets are considered degrading activities, and by all accounts induce a profound horror among all 'well-born' Hindus. Gandhi decided to grapple head-on with this issue. He personally cleaned toilets and chamber pots. He made cleaning them an integral part of the compulsory routine in his ashrams for all inmates (Gandhi, 2001). With his wife, he appears to have been harsher. In his autobiography, he reveals that he lost his temper with his wife Kasturba, not for her refusing to clean the chamber pot of a visiting guest, who, unsurprisingly, was himself a member of a ritually untouchable caste, but that she did not perform her task with a smile on her face (Gandhi, 2001). What was behind this obsession with toilet cleaning? Gandhi correctly identified this activity as an overwhelmingly important *identity marker* that set apart the so-called untouchables from upper-caste Hindus. He therefore rightly concluded that unless this connection was broken, attempts to integrate the untouchable castes into the larger Hindu and Indian folds must fail. Just as in our earlier example—women are supposed to stay at home and raise children—persons classified as untouchables were supposed to clean privies.

Clearly, the reformer Gandhi belonged to the camp that rejected such anti-feminist and casteist positions. Gandhi insisted that all who sought his association and approbation would have to do the same. This drives a nail into this ancient and persistent identity problem. Working with leather, which after all is cured animal skin/hide, is also considered polluting; and again, in the traditional paradigm, this activity is reserved for the untouchable castes. Gandhi insisted that leatherwork, particularly the making of leather shoes and slippers, be included in ashram activities. Curiously, despite being against vivisection and a defender of animal rights in other contexts (CW, 1999, v. 44, p. 267), Gandhi was a supporter of leatherwork for himself and his associates. Again, the reason for this interest seems to be connected with his desire to invalidate caste identities. When it came to religious identity, Gandhi had a more difficult task. India was partitioned on largely religious lines. Gandhi considered this his personal failure. He got around the issue of religious identity, not by asking people to give up their faiths, which would in any event have not been practical. Instead, he held daily prayer meetings where prayers and hymns of all religions were included. Here was an attempt to create an overarching human religious identity without jettisoning sectarian ones. Sheean points out that Gandhi fell back on grappling with pollution issues even while dealing with religious identity. For traditional Hindus, there are religious taboos associated with accepting food from other castes. Gandhi broke many of his fasts by accepting a glass of fruit juice from Muslims (Sheean, 2005). Even in the world of R.K. Narayan's fiction, the Mahatma accepts food from a poor untouchable boy rather than from a rich upper-caste man (Narayan, 2010). Even in this fictional account, the Mahatma's action is meant as a message to the upper castes.

It is interesting to remember that Gandhi used his identity as a political prisoner in a South African jail to undertake, as part of his allotted prison work, the making of a pair of sandals, which he then presented to his political opponent, the prim and proper General Smuts. The idea of fluid identities could not have been better demonstrated. To his credit, General Smuts retained the sandals as one of the most treasured gifts that life itself had bestowed on him.

Nudging Identities

Identities are not frozen. Norms and their social contexts have a direct impact on the formation of identities. Akerlof and Kranton spend a considerable amount of time looking at the behavioural consequences of something as arcane as the 'honour code' at the US military academy at West Point. The motivation to adhere to this code can quite easily be fitted even into Nobel laureate Gary Becker's neoclassical paradigm of including so-called non-economic motivations in utility functions (Becker, 2010). Dharmic considerations of virtue linked to identities could very well be matters that proverbially rational, selfish, utility-maximizing economic agents would want to optimize. A neat, practical way out to push one's ethical framework, if ever there was one! This brings us to the Nobel laureate behavioural economist Richard Thaler's concept of the 'nudge' (Thaler and Sunstein 2010). Simply speaking, can people be nudged along in a direction that changes their norms, and hence the way they identify themselves and the way they would like to be identified by others? Akerlof and Kranton look for identity definitions having a starting point—e.g., teenager, woman, African American, employee, and so on—but they are emphatic in pointing out that norms can and do change and that this results in changes in identities. They make reference to the dramatic conclusions of Muzafer Sherif's foundational Robber's Cave experiment, which showed that identities can be easily acquired and can be endowed with disproportionate importance (Akerlof and Kramton, 2010).

In this famous experiment, two groups of young boys were divided in a completely random manner in a trekking/hiking camp. With minimal nudges, the two groups were easily persuaded to become aggressive, even violent adversaries. When the nudges and messages were changed, the two groups of boys came together as friends. Thaler and his colleague Sunstein argue that nudges that result in changing norms can be made without any element of compulsion or excessive paternalism (Thaler and Sunstein, 2010).

Gandhi would have approved of this. He abhorred the use of force. He was opposed to statutes 'imposed from above' (CW, 1999, v. 98, p. 14). But he would not have been satisfied with a morally neutral approach, however benign the intentions. The nudge would necessarily have to be in a morally worthwhile direction. And here he would be guided by the still small inner voice of conscience (CW, 1999, v. 76, p. 349), much as the father of economics, Adam Smith, would have pointed in the direction of the impartial spectator (Smith, 2002). Becker, Akerlof, Kranton, Thaler and Sunstein are practitioners of positive economics in the sense defined by Milton Friedman (1953). Positive economics is focused on theories that best explain actual empirical data until another theory comes along that explains the same data better. Gandhi is closer to Smith in stressing the normative and moral dimensions. Writing in *Young India* on 20 August 1925, he openly admits as follows: 'I have sought the friendship of the capitalists in order to induce them to regard themselves as trustees' (Gandhi, 1965). When a person with the charisma of the Mahatma 'induces' someone to do something, it must be quite difficult to resist. In his interview with *Modern Review* in October 1935, Gandhi's responses could very well be read as precursors to the descriptions of the development of norms and identities as viewed by scholars of today. Gandhi says: 'While admitting that man actually lives by habit, I hold it is better for him to live by the exercise of will.' The importance of conscious human agency is assumed and emphasized in a tone that suggests that counterarguments are not worth taking seriously. And, almost immediately, he seems to anticipate the fear that nudges may result in forcible state intervention. 'I look upon an increase of the power of the state with the greatest fear . . . it does the greatest harm to mankind by destroying individuality, which lies at the root of all progress.' And then he delivers the coup-de-grace, upholding the moral potential of individuals, while almost casually but emphatically registering a damning indictment of the state as an institution detrimental to the poor. 'We know of so many cases where men have adopted trusteeship, but none where the State has really lived for the poor' (*Modern Review*, 1935; CW, 1999, v. 65, p. 319). This reads almost like something from a libertarian tract, albeit one focused on the inherent morality of one's approach to the poor, reminding one of Gandhi's much-loved Gospels of Mark and Matthew.

There exist multiple ways in which human agency can be exercised, norms changed, and primordial identities altered. Women can be told, for instance, that in order to succeed in the workplace, they should adopt male norms and imitate male identities. A case can be made that in order to achieve social and economic 'success', African Americans should be encouraged to imitate the whites. In Gandhi's youth, it was accepted as a self-evident truth that Indians would gain not just economically but also morally by imitating their British rulers. *Hind Swaraj* can be seen as a strong criticism of this method or practice of changing norms and identities. Gandhi's clear message was that such a chameleon-like identity change would be disastrous for Indians (Parel, HS, 2009). What he emphasized was the need for Indians and the British to seek to move norms towards universal and eternal verities common to the best in both cultures. Merely because brutal British and Boer imperialists had stopped believing in the norms of their own Christian faith did not mean that Gandhi, the brown Hindu Indian, could not lay claim to the message embedded in the Gospels (Nandy, 2009; Nandy, 2013). And Gandhi applied a sense of symmetry to normative and identity discourses among his own countrymen and countrywomen.

Kolge points out that in the early twentieth century, it was not uncommon for upper-caste Hindu reformers to appeal to lower-caste persons to abandon polluting acts and become ritually pure. Gandhi inverted this message. He asked his upper-caste compatriots to take up polluting and ritually impure activities in order to end the markers of identity differentiators (Kolge, 2017). Gandhi had a similar position on gender identities. Ashis Nandy makes the case that European imperialism in general and British imperialism in particular were imbued with a culture of hyper-masculinity, which was tinged with a sentimental attachment to 'manly' boarding-school identities. The imperial ideology posited that manliness implied courage and strength—virtues possessed by the ruling white race. The conquered Indians could improve themselves only when they shed their effeminate traits. They would then cease to be cowardly and weak. Gandhi did not simply question this world view; he rejected it completely. Humanity's feminine part was not to be suppressed, but embraced and celebrated. And far from being associated with weakness or cowardice, it was associated with bravery, resilience, deep strength and a nurturing creativity. By downplaying the feminine within themselves and in their societies, by abandoning any hopes of creative androgyny, it was India's British rulers who were the losers and who perhaps would benefit from revisiting their norms and their gender identity constructs (Nandy, 2009). Feminists, economists and psychologists could make use of this striking insight of the Mahatma's to make the case for a relook at gender identity markers and their role in the political economy of the workplace, and whether this might actually not contribute to productivity and quality gains. Thaler and his associates could constructively consider whether nudges that result in the reduction of hyper-masculine behaviour patterns may not lead to a more peaceful and vibrant economy.

Max Weber was an admirer of Protestant Christianity and felt that Indian progress had been retarded on account of Hindu philosophical and social norms. Despite Max Weber's disdain for

Hindu traditions, it turns out that there are strong parallels between Weber and Gandhi as they independently developed doctrines of worldly asceticism (Scott, 2016). Akerlof and Kranton too get inspiration from Weber as they take a look at office-holders. When faced only with 'monetary rewards and economic goals, they will game the system'. On the other hand, when imbued with norms that define a fiduciary identity, their behaviour changes and 'conflicts of interest' tend to get dissipated (Akerlof and Kranton, 2010). Gandhi's approach was quite similar, despite or perhaps because it emanated from religious maxims. Human beings, especially the wealthy, who according to the Gospels have a low probability of salvation, needed to be nudged to take the position that they were not reckless, imperious hyper-masculine owners of wealth but sober, sensitive, nurturing trustees of wealth, and that their wealth was held in trust for the Lord, the Lord's people, typically the poor and future generations. And just as Gandhi challenged the British rulers to reach back to the best in themselves, not only because this would be good for India, but because it would restore a wholeness to the British themselves, adoption of the trustee identity is not just in order to help the poor, it is necessary in order to liberate and embellish the rich.

10

Tinkering and the Mahatma: Gandhi's Ideas on Education[*]

The Economics of Human Capital

Adam Smith, in his *Wealth of Nations*, draws our attention to the idea of 'useful abilities' acquired by human beings as being a fundamental feature that is essential for the emergence of economic activity and economic welfare (Smith, 1982). In that sense, Smith once more, as is his habit with virtually every aspect of economics, stands anointed as the father of human capital economics, a field which had been referred to by A.C. Pigou (1928), but which gained currency later in the last century with Becker (1994), Mincer (1958), Lewis (1954) and Schultz (1961) as its principal expositors. These economists have focused on the importance of skills, education and health of the populations of different societies and the importance of these factors in propelling or hindering economic growth.

In his brilliant introductions in the 1997 and 2009 editions of Gandhi's *Hind Swaraj* (Parel, HS, 2009), Professor Anthony

---

[*] A shortened, summarized variant of this chapter has been converted into a standalone paper jointly authored by Shishir Jha and myself.

Parel makes it clear that Gandhi was concerned with the physical, educational, mental, moral and spiritual development of his fellow-Indians. Though he was primarily addressing his own compatriots in *Hind Swaraj*, the Mahatma was implicitly reaching out to all humans. Here may lie the first germ of Gandhi's tryst with the economics of human capital. To put it simply, *Hind Swaraj* demonstrates that Gandhi shares with Smith his concern for 'human abilities', an expression which sounds prosaic, but which is pregnant with extensive possibilities and hints of promise.

Gandhi's Intellectual Sources

Gandhi's contributions to the subject of development of 'human abilities', like all his other intellectual interventions, had multiple sources. His idealized Indian village and villager were, of course, central inspirations. Jewish friends like Kallenbach and Frydman stand out as important contributors to the Mahatma's thought processes and actions in this area. The polychromatic J.C. Kumarappa—economist, accountant and incandescent religious thinker, all rolled into one—can be said to have simultaneously both influenced Gandhi and been influenced by him. Christian sources had influenced Gandhi in his religious and political views, and economics was not an exception. After all, Gandhi had referred to Christ as 'the greatest economist of his time' (CW, 1999, v. 15, p. 275). The Christian influences came from multiple directions. Catholic Trappist monks and Protestant Pietist activists are prominent in the list. Gandhi came up with his own suggestions as to how education should be conceived, offered and pursued. This resulted in the Nai Talim or New Learning movement. The imprint of the psychologist and pedagogical expert Maria Montessori is quite clear in Gandhi's conceptual framework for Nai Talim.

As Parel repeatedly points out, the Mahatma was emphatic about the need for human beings to be engaged with one another. Not for him the lonely anchorite existence. In the final analysis, it is

Gandhi's directly lived experience in the communities of the Phoenix Settlement and Tolstoy Farm in South Africa and in the Sabarmati Ashram in India that gave him the inputs and insights which shaped his ideas and plans. It is easy to dismiss these communities as wannabe utopias without a self-sustaining character. This has been the criticism by V.S. Naipaul, who on balance is a detached admirer of the Mahatma (Naipaul, 2012; Naipaul, 1990). While Naipaul may be partially correct, he misses the wider ramifications of Gandhi's experiments. Gandhi managed to understand that the development of 'human abilities' along Smithian lines involved both solitary and community pursuits. It is important to take note of the Mahatma's love for spinning, praying and meditating in solitude, along with his penchant for singing and gardening in groups. The need for combining the activities of solitary individuals and teams imbued with solidarity is taken for granted in modern human capital economics (Becker, 1994). It is to Gandhi's credit that in some sense he anticipated this need to combine the binaries.

While the moral training required for the pursuit of a non-violent political protest movement remains of enduring interest to political philosophers, we may wish to focus our attention on other aspects of Gandhi's contributions to human capital economics. We should not forget that the dismemberment of the British Empire in India was for Gandhi a necessary, but by no means sufficient, condition for the eventual goal of improvement of the lot of Indians. But just because Gandhi was a moralist, it does not mean that he was not interested in the practical improvement and development of all Indians and by extension, all humans. His assertion in his 1916 Allahabad speech that 'grinding pauperism' leads to 'moral degradation' would in fact suggest to us that it was precisely because he was a moralist seeking to avoid 'moral degradation' that he was interested in liberating Indians from poverty. This task involved paying attention to their human capital development.

As is clear in *Hind Swaraj*, Gandhi, like many thinking Indians of his time, had bought into the theory of 'economic drain' propounded by Dadabhai Naoroji (Naoroji, 2010) and R.C. Dutt (Dutt, 2013), which argued that contemporary Indian poverty was a direct result of egregiously high taxation by the British in order to fund activities not directly connected with Indian matters (e.g., wars in Abyssinia and China), and that British trade and exchange rate policies were harshly mercantilist and sought disproportionate gains for British manufacturers and operated against the interests of Indian producers and consumers. But the really brilliant feature of *Hind Swaraj* is its enormous and enduring concern not so much with how imperialists behave, but with the agency of Indians themselves. On the political plane, Gandhi argued it was the support of Indians—especially those who were explicitly or implicitly beneficiaries of British rule economically and those who were culturally over-impressed with British rule—that was the problem. In his inimitable style, he turned away from angry victimhood to the issue of agency of the so-called victims.

Indians needed to be liberated from their 'pauperism'. So, where does one start? A decade before Gandhi's return to India, the 'Swadeshi' movement had pioneered the idea of boycotting foreign products and favouring Indian products. Gandhi is now confronted with this issue. We need to remember that in *Hind Swaraj*, he has already expressed his disquiet with modern industrialism. So, he has to decide whether he is against all industrial products or only against British products. In his typical way, Gandhi works out a solution, which needs to be viewed as much in the context of his actions as within the penumbra of his all-too-extravagant words.

As it turns out, neither in his politics nor in his economics was Gandhi willing to let matters rest by simply blaming the British. Just as in the political sphere he kept asserting in *Hind Swaraj* that it was Indian cooperation that sustained imperialism, he was focused quite pointedly on what Indians can do (as against simply blaming others) about their wretched 'pauperism'. The issue of agency—both individual and collective—never left the Mahatma's range of concerns. His erudite interlocutor Parel understands this and repeatedly points it out (Parel, HS, 2009). Gandhi cleverly went back to engaging with the textile industry. The emerging narrative in India was that the British had deliberately and consciously decimated the Indian weaver in order for their mills in Manchester to do well. The apocryphal story of cruel British agents chopping off the thumbs of Dacca weavers in order to throttle Indian textiles is widely circulated and remains an enduring image in the minds of Indian schoolchildren to this day. The Swadeshi movement that had started in 1905 had already made the case for preferring Indian products over British products. As was to be expected of him, Gandhi decided to go one step forward. He railed against cloth from Manchester; but simultaneously, he vigorously embraced an anti-industrial and an anti-machine position (providing immense support to his *Hind Swaraj* arguments) as he ended up advocating hand-spinning and hand-weaving. Instead of complaining about their wretched condition, if India's poor started spinning yarn with a hand-tool, they could actually generate an income stream that would, in part at least, make them less poor.

And Then Came the Charkha

The hand-tool used for spinning yarn had actually disappeared from common usage. It is a tribute to Gandhi's genius that he literally 're-discovered' what he went on to christen as the 'charkha'. This was a primitive, rudimentary spinning wheel which required no steam, no electricity, no sophisticated modern paraphernalia. (The connection with his *Hind Swaraj* scepticism about the spinning jennies which heralded the beginnings of British imperial power is subliminally indicated.) Anyone could learn how to use the charkha. She could take the cotton so readily available in India and spin yarn from it. It is tempting to keep going back to the verb 'spin' when we analyse what Gandhi was propagating. The political metaphor was that Indians could spin their way to freedom. The economic metaphor was that Indians could spin their way out of poverty or pauperism, if you prefer. In the succeeding years, Gandhi convinced millions of his followers that they should spin yarn on the charkha. He made it mandatory for those who wished to call themselves his disciples or acolytes. Very soon, he got the charkha to become a central symbol on the very potent flag used by the Indian National Congress. The charkha ceased to be an optional hand-tool. It was now a talisman of sorts.

At the end of all this, two intriguing questions remain. If the entire doctrine of evil British mercantilism and the cruel act of cutting off the thumbs of Dacca weavers were not to be upheld, then why focus on spinning and not on weaving? I believe that therein lies an understanding of Gandhi's rather unique (words like 'quixotic' or 'bizarre' are inappropriate, as the succeeding analysis will show) understanding of the development of human capital. Gandhi certainly advocated hand-weaving and the handloom as the appropriate tool. But nowhere in his writings do we find the almost lyrical association he had with spinning when it comes to weaving. The responses to this conundrum lie both in the realms of realpolitik and in what quite crucially might involve Gandhi's concern with human agency and the broader insights he has produced for us in the field of the economics of human capital. It is interesting to examine the trajectory of Gandhi's life and involvements in this context.

Spinning versus Weaving

On his return to India, Gandhi could have chosen to settle down in Porbandar, where he was born, or in Bombay, whose citizens seemed inordinately fond of this South African returnee. His choice of Ahmedabad is quite interesting.

Porbandar would have cramped him. Firstly, it was too small and too unimportant a place for a man who had large aspirations and ambitions, such as taking on the most powerful empire in the world. But there was an even more proximate reason, given that Gandhi was primarily interested in political action. One of the amazing and inexplicable features of British rule in India was that free speech and free, even modestly incendiary political activity, had better legal protection in those parts of India directly ruled by the British than in the territories indirectly controlled by the British, where the Indian Maharajas and Nawabs were formally in charge. In Porbandar, the endlessly verbose Mahatma would have been silenced. His political activity, even of the most non-violent and anodyne kind, would simply have not been permitted by the local Maharaja even as the potentate and his courtiers operated under the stern guidance of a schoolmasterly British official.

Bombay would have been another logical choice. It was the birthplace of the Indian National Congress, the leading national political organization of the time. Bombay was a politically active place and it was quite hospitable and welcoming as far as Gandhi was concerned. But Bombay had its disadvantages. In Durban and Johannesburg, Gandhi had blossomed in an environment where Indians from different regions living in the shadow of the British Empire had managed to acquire and assert a synthesized Indian identity. From that perspective, Bombay was similar. It was a heterogeneous mosaic of different religious and linguistic groups. For Gandhi, this was a plus. As one who had defended the composite Indian persona in South Africa, he was popular with all groups. But Bombay's cosmopolitanism and modernity were also negatives, from Gandhi's perspective. He was consciously seeking a renewed tryst with his roots. This was also in keeping with the advice given to him by his political guru, Gopal Krishna Gokhale, who had advised the returnee from South Africa to get to know the proverbial real India. Bombay was far from being the real India. Additionally, it could even be thought of as a Portuguese and British creation, not an authentically Indian location. Uncharitable critics would argue that in Bombay, Gandhi may have been outshone by other stalwart political leaders. There may be an element of truth in this point of view. But when one looks at the sheer quantum of political adulation and financial support that Gandhi got over the next several decades from the people of Bombay, it seems unlikely that this concern, however valid, would have deterred the intrepid putative Mahatma. In search of his roots, or perhaps to ensure his rootedness, Gandhi turned to a city in his native Gujarat north of Bombay, but still within the same province as Bombay: Ahmedabad.

Even within the constraints described above, Ahmedabad was by no means Gandhi's only choice. Surat was definitely an option. From a historical perspective, it would have been the ultimate irony for the inveterate adversary of the British Raj in India to settle down in Surat, where, after all, the English East India Company began its operations some centuries ago and laid the foundations for the empire that was to follow. But Surat had gone downhill over time. Its port had silted because of the vagaries of the Tapi River. Its most entrepreneurial people had moved on to flourishing Bombay. Ahmedabad, in interior Gujarat, was also of pre-British vintage; but it was quite different. Unlike Surat, which had only been a Moghul port, even if an important one, Ahmedabad had the distinction of being the capital of the earlier Gujarat sultanate. Instead of going into a downward spiral, Ahmedabad had actually witnessed a growth spurt in the nineteenth century. And churlish observers might make the point that Ahmedabad had no towering political leaders who might be competitive thorns in Gandhi's side. In any event, Gandhi chose Ahmedabad. This choice was not without its ironies and challenges, which are worth examining.

Ahmedabad was a city trying hard to industrialize. It was in fact trying to do pretty much what Gandhi had been negative about in *Hind Swaraj* (Parel, HS, 2009). It was attempting to be everything other than an idyllic village. But that was only half the story. Ahmedabad had leaped on to the bandwagon of the modern textile industry and was getting studded with textile mills, which were being set up in large numbers. The Ahmedabad textile industry was the antithesis and adversary of handloom. To make matters worse, Gandhi emerged as a friend of the textile industry. Leading textile magnates like Ambalal Sarabhai and Kasturbhai Lalbhai were

Gandhi's supporters in multiple contexts. Their financial backing of Gandhi and his activities were of considerable significance. Gandhi was also intimately connected with the mill workers of Ahmedabad. He even led a workers' strike against the magnates, such contradictory friendships and associations being par for the course for the enigmatic Mahatma. How, then, was Gandhi going to support handloom and oppose mills, if that would result in alienating investors and workers who depended on modern textile mills? Perhaps here lies the realpolitik answer to Gandhi's loud and vociferous advocacy of spinning and his more muted support for weaving.

I would argue that this realpolitik explanation fails to take into account Gandhi's crucial insight in the field of human capital development. In our analysis of Gandhi's engagement with identity economics, we have examined the Mahatma's approach to caste, as brilliantly explored by Nishikant Kolge (Kolge, 2017). It was important for Gandhi to attempt to redirect the identities of Indians away from disdain for manual labour, which was an activity reserved not for upper-caste persons, but for members of the lower castes. Spinning was an admirable answer. It quite ably addressed Gandhi's concern for introducing manual labour to Indians as a dignified and worthwhile pursuit. While the identity and dignity issues are certainly relevant, this writer would argue that the consequential advantages of spinning were far more profound. Spinning involved the direct use of one's hands and fingers. These characteristics of spinning made it not just any activity, but one which had education, skill development and the resultant human capital development as its goal. The Italian pedagogical pioneer Maria Montessori had independently arrived at the conclusion that activity and engagement with physical objects improved childhood educational outcomes much better than the proverbial blackboard or notebook. We know that Gandhi and Montessori met several times and were quite friendly. Gandhi visited Montessori's school during his visit to England for the Round Table Conference. The principal agenda at that time seems to have been education and promotion of world peace. But it is pretty safe to assume that Gandhi was acquainted with and supportive of Montessori's approach to education. As we will presently examine, Gandhi's own Nai Talim or New Learning plans were almost derivative of Montessori's theories in many ways.

Gandhi's extraordinarily high-decibel emphasis on spinning, as against his relatively muted support for weaving, also makes sense when we take into account that fact that the spinning wheel or charkha was a low-cost hand-tool. A handloom was a much bigger piece of equipment requiring a much larger space. In practical terms, the development of motor skills, eye-hand co-ordination and what modern neuroscientists refer to as left- and right-brain balance can be explored easily and cheaply by spinning rather than by weaving. In his foundational text, *Gandhi's Economic Thought*, Ajit Dasgupta presents an interesting argument that Adam Smith and the Mahatma were on the same page when it came to the subject of the efficiencies derived from the division of labour. To quote Dasgupta, 'Gandhi strongly opposed the proposal that cotton spinners should also be encouraged to weave, for he believed that this involved economic disadvantage' (Dasgupta, 1996)—division of labour emerges as one more resounding reason to keep the focus relentlessly and emphatically on spinning.

From Spinning to Tinkering

In a striking and unexpected way, Gandhi seems to have wanted his countrymen and countrywomen to become not just spinners, but tinkerers. The historian Corelli Barnett has pointed out that the education system introduced by the British in India was not only selective and elitist (the colonial bureaucrats were perfectly fine if the majority of Indians remained illiterate), but it was excessively focused on academic disciplines like literature, history, philosophy and law. There was less emphasis on technical subjects, and there was no attempt at creating any serious apprenticeship curriculum (Barnett, 2011). The overwhelming majority among the leaders of the Indian Freedom movement were lawyers; there were a couple of doctors; engineers were conspicuously absent. While there were exceptions like M. Visveswarayya, most of the admittedly small number of engineers that British India did produce tended to be of the classroom and office variety. The British did not set up institutions like the US Land Grant colleges. There was no attempt at setting up a technical apprentice system on German lines. Meiji Japan invited Americans like William Wheeler, whose expertise was engineering and agriculture and who went on to become the president of Sapporo Agricultural College, now better known as Hokkaido University. The analogous person in British India who became the vice chancellor of Calcutta University was Sir Henry Maine, an eminent historian of law. Barnett's argument is clearly well supported.

Consciously or otherwise, Gandhi with his charkha was creating a backdoor apprenticeship programme, where manual labour and tinkering skills were a significant by-product. The beauty of Gandhi's charkha was that while pursuing the goal of spinning their way to political freedom, his followers were also set to acquire the attitudes, the skills and the approaches that could lead them to greater technical agility, and ironically to a more fruitful engagement with machines, even though ostensibly machines were objects of Gandhi's dislike, as articulated in *Hind Swaraj* (Parel, HS, 2009). The spinning wheel, the charkha, was after all a machine, was it not?

The Trappist Influence

Before we go on to examining some of the lesser-known aspects of the Mahatma's peculiar relationship with machines, be they spinning wheels, printing presses or sewing machines, it is important to delve into certain influences that he grappled with well before he met Montessori. While in South Africa, Gandhi visited the Trappist monastery outside Durban. This monastery had been established by the Mariannhill congregation of the Trappists. Gandhi was impressed by the austere Christian holiness of the monks. He was also impressed by the commitment of the monks to manual labour. The noted Gandhian Tridib Suhrud has examined the Trappist influence on Gandhi, which led to Gandhi's lifelong concerns with prayer, with silence, with 'working with the hands' and with gardening (as Professor Suhrud mentioned in his inimitable way to me in 2014, we must not forget that Mendel, the father of genetics, was after all a monk and a gardening enthusiast!). In more ways than one, the Trappist influence pervaded Gandhi's own 'ashrams', the places where he and his followers were to lead a collective existence. Prayer, mandatory silence, 'lowly' work and chastity, all come to mind. Of special interest to us is the emphasis on solitude. It turns out that spinning is an activity that can be done in solitude, and is perhaps best done in solitude. Meditation and prayer are ideal mental practices that can accompany the physical act of spinning. That this prayerful and spiritually elevating activity contributed to India's national freedom movement and also improved the fine motor skills of his followers must, from the Mahatma's point of view, to have seemed not accidental, but obvious and divinely ordained.

Gandhi's direct interest in physical labour was not restricted to spinning. His friend, partner, supporter and collaborator in South Africa, Hermann Kallenbach, was a reasonably good carpenter. He taught carpentry skills to the group of volunteers who gathered around Gandhi in the Tolstoy Farm 'ashram', which the two of them set up outside Johannesburg on land donated by Kallenbach. And again, a Trappist connection is made. This time by the unlikely agency of Kallenbach, who himself was of Lithuanian-Jewish origin. Kallenbach learned shoe-making from Trappist monks, and in turn taught it to the residents of Tolstoy Farm (CW,1999, v. 72, p. 349) We have already noted how and why leatherwork and shoe-making were important lower-caste-untouchable identity markers in Indian society. Clearly, Gandhi was trying to subvert this identity doctrine. We have examined this subject in an earlier chapter. Carpentry and shoe-making are also ideal 'tinkering' activities, substantiating the argument that by intent or otherwise, Gandhi's actions and message remain pregnant with important implications in the realm of human capital development. When it came to leatherwork and shoe-making, Gandhi extended his interests, and by implication his desired direction, to show how this activity can lead to higher levels of abstraction in the tinkering process. There was a considerable amount of discussion between the Mahatma and his favourite economist, the redoubtable J.C. Kumarappa, on the ideal design of a sturdy sandal that would be suited to the hot and humid conditions of India (Redkar, 2019). We will presently come back to the powerful idea that physical labour leads to tinkering, which then leads to design experiments not just with footwear but also with the Mahatma's beloved charkha.

Gandhi and Machines

It would be useful to revisit Gandhi's engagement with machines. Reading *Hind Swaraj*, one cannot but be left with the impression that Gandhi was opposed to machines, large-scale industrialization, and large factories. Nevertheless, there is sufficient evidence to show that Gandhi was not simplistic, rigid or closed-minded in his approach to machines. Gandhi was a journalist and a newspaper editor, and it is noteworthy that Gandhi was also a printer who worked and operated his own printing press, a wondrous machine in its own right. Gandhi operated printing presses himself in the Phoenix Settlement near Durban, in Tolstoy Farm near Johannesburg, and in Sabarmati Ashram in Ahmedabad. The fact that he personally knew how to operate the printing press demonstrates Gandhi's direct intimacy and interaction with machines; it was not a theoretical armchair acquaintance.

Gandhi has gone on record to say that he was a lover of the sewing machine and an admirer of its inventor Fredrick Singer (CW, 1999, v. 29, p. 266). Gandhi wrongly attributed Singer's invention to the inventor's intention to save his wife from tedium. In fact, Singer was a notorious philanderer and his invention was not even remotely associated with any affection for his wife (Jones and

Kiron, 2017). But the key thing to note is Gandhi's concern for the relief that the sewing machine provided to the hard-working and hard-hit housewife. Just as Gandhi wished to relieve Indians from their 'grinding pauperism', he was all for reduction in the grinding tedium of overly hard labour. He had argued in *Hind Swaraj* against machines, among other reasons because they displaced human labour (Parel, HS, 2009). And yet, when it came to the sewing machine, such displacement (after all, one person using the machine could sew as many garments as many persons without the machine) provided this machine provided relief to the worker.

Running through *Hind Swaraj* is a recurring theme which is less about the traditional trade-unionist's objection to machines because of potential job displacement. It is more of a quasi-mystical concern that excessive machinery may result in human beings becoming quite simply, dehumanized. The human-machine relationship and its effect on the human psyche are subjects of extensive study by psychologists. Gandhi's concern seems to emanate from his intuitive fear of what machines may do to us at a subliminal level. The question of who is to be the master is a recurring one in science fiction. While not being a science fiction writer, Gandhi certainly had a prophetic strain in him. Gandhi's prescience and his love for the sewing machine, which presumably enhanced the quality of life of the user, can be seen as precursors to the late twentieth-century obsessions with user-friendliness and easy interface, which have become mantras for product designers.

Hind Swaraj needs to be read as a high-level statement of concern about modern civilization, especially its epiphenomenon of imperialism and the consequent pauperism of many, including Gandhi's fellow-Indian citizens. It would not be proper to pick on every detail in the book and marshal clever and petty arguments to run down Gandhi as a reactionary Luddite. This is especially the case when we consider Gandhi's actions. He was quite comfortable with being judged by his actions. Gandhi used the railways extensively, although he was conscious that railways may encourage what he considered unnecessary and frivolous travel. He was also concerned about the propensity of railways to spread disease (CW, 1999, v. 10, p. 267). Recent pandemic phenomena, which have been exacerbated by an octopus-like travel industry, might give us reason to not reject this line of argument entirely.

Gandhi used the telegraph and radio extensively. This might come from his willingness to constantly and continually expose himself to information and intellectual currents from all over the world. After all, he had gone on record to say that he was not going to close the doors of his mind to such winds (CW, 1999, v. 23, p. 15). Gandhi's practical empiricism always trumped some of the high-sounding positions of *Hind Swaraj*, even though he refused till his last days to disavow that seminal text. In his public meetings, Gandhi willingly made use of loudspeakers, which were clearly products of factories. Gandhi moved quite effortlessly from the printing press to the radio in his later years. Given his soft, hoarse voice, his radio talks have ended up becoming extraordinary examples of credible and endearing communication. Clearly, here the Mahatma was the master of the medium and the machine, not the other way around!

Nowhere is Gandhi's love affair with machines better seen than in his engagement with the spinning wheel, the charkha. He was constantly tinkering with it to make it more efficient, more user-friendly for the spinner, lighter and easier to deal with. In this endeavour, the Mahatma enlisted the talents of an unlikely Polish Jew, Maurice Frydman. Frydman was an engineer who had relocated to India on the invitation of Mirza Ismail, the diwan or prime minister of the princely state of Mysore. Frydman's first assignment was to set up a factory in Mysore. Frydman belonged to the inter-war eclectic European Jewish intelligentsia who had diverse interests. Frydman fell in love with Gandhian political thought and he worked on writing a Constitution for village republics. He even got a chance at attempting to implement his utopian ideas in Aundh in western India. Needless to say, the Mahatma encouraged him quite a bit in this endeavour. And then Frydman returned to his first love: engineering. He embarked on a career improving the designs of agricultural implements, tools and simple machines. Gandhi got him to take a look at the charkha. Frydman successfully improved the design of the traditional charkha to make it more efficient and usable (CW, 1999, v. 80, p. 104; v. 81, p. 170; Frydman, 1944). To use modern marketing jargon, Frydman had come up with a new, improved charkha! The Mahatma was delighted with the efforts of his disciple. When India got its independence, perhaps the only unusual request Gandhi made to the government of the country, which referred to him as the Father of the Nation, was to ask it to confer Indian citizenship on Frydman (Akbar, 2020). The multi-talented Polish Jew, whose entire family perished in the European holocaust, received the hospitality of a tolerant, welcoming, grateful India. He spent his last days as a proud Indian, and died as one.

Gandhi was not a frozen-in-time lover of an idyllic and non-existent past. His desire to improve the charkha and his gratification when that happened shows him up almost as a Burkean conservative committed to gradual, incremental change. It is also not the case that he was only a votary of small machines and not of big factories. He was forever pragmatic and situational in his responses, as long as fundamental verities like truth and non-violence were not at stake. Shipping was one area where British companies jealously guarded their entrenched positions. Enormous legal and other hurdles were put in place to prevent Indian businesses from gaining entry into this British preserve. At the turn of the century, the south Indian entrepreneur V.O. Chidambaram was hounded, persecuted and even jailed for his temerity to set up a shipping line. In the thirties of the twentieth century, when the Scindia Company launched a ship under an Indian flag, Gandhi's pride knew no bounds and he publicly welcomed and celebrated this event (CW, 1999, v. 39, p. 335). Gandhi was certainly aware that the ship concerned had not been built in a village smithy, but in a large modern shipyard. This did not deter him from expressing his support and his joy. William Shirer has written about Gandhi's reaction when he visited the textile mills of Lancashire in the thirties of the twentieth century. Gandhi was appalled at the antique and obsolescent condition of the machinery in the Manchester mills and commented with quiet pride that the mills in his native Ahmedabad were far more modern, efficient and attractive. Here again, one sees no great dislike for large factories per se. Gandhi was knowledgeable enough to tell the difference between a decaying factory and an up-to-date one. If anything, he admired modernity when it suggested efficiency at the same time (Shirer, 1980).

The Philosophy behind Nai Talim: Montessori, Kumarappa

So, what then was Gandhi's prescription for wholesome human capital development in his country? He called it Nai Talim, or New Learning. Like Corelli Barnett, Gandhi was opposed to an excessively theoretical and academic system of education, which was the norm in British India (Barnett, 2011). As we have discussed, Gandhi was committed to tinkering for multiple reasons. Spinning on the charkha not only involved Montessori's concern with motor skills and enhanced learning, but also contributed to acquisition of the disciplines of silence and meditation. Music and gardening were instrumental in the development of skills associated with the modern expression, teamwork. Gandhi was a moralist. But he was also an empiricist. So even morality had to be inculcated among the students in a practical manner. All these considerations and some more went into the conceptualization and design of Nai Talim. Of Gandhi's many suggestions and plans, the ones associated with Nai Talim or New Learning are perhaps the most ignored in independent India. It is by no means clear that Indian human capital development has not been the loser for it.

The Catholic Trappist monks had inspired Gandhi and had earned his admiration. They had also transmitted skills which he and his followers had leveraged. In his development of a lived community learning experience, consciously or otherwise, Gandhi was treading in the path of another Christian congregation. In this context it was a Protestant Lutheran Pietist group. The Danish Pietist, Bartholomaeus Ziegenbalg, had established the first Tamil printing press in Tarangambadi (Tranquebar) in the early 1700s. The Mahatma, who opposed active proselytization and conversion by Christian missionaries (CW, 1999, v. 68, p. 20), would have considered Ziegenbalg the ideal 'good' Christian. Ziegenbalg '. . . showed a deep respect for Hindu traditions and tried to avoid presenting Christianity in woodenly Western terms. His resolution to discuss his faith thoughtfully with Muslims and Hindus took precedence for him over seeking rapid conversions' (MacCulloch, 2010). Ziegenbalg obtained support from the English Anglican Society for promoting Christian knowledge in a clearly unusual ecumenical gesture across denominations. The Society sent a printing press to Tranquebar. A pioneering translation of the Bible into Tamil was the result. In the 1730s, Count Nikolaus Ludwig von Zinzendorf, a nobleman from Saxony in Germany, introduced another Christian influence, that of the Moravians, in Tranquebar (MacCulloch, 2010).

Zieganbalg and his successor, Christian Fredrick Schwartz, had an indirect influence on the development of Gandhi's ideas in economics and education through the personality of Joseph Chelladurai Kumarappa (often referred to as J.C. Kumarappa or simply JCK). In the 1700s, the Protestant mission out of Tranquebar adopted an unusual strategy (not that unusual actually, as the Catholic Jesuit de Nobili had tried something similar a century earlier in Madurai) of obtaining patronage and support from the Hindu king of Tanjavur—which was adjacent to Tranquebar—and of engaging respectfully with upper-caste Hindus. Out of this fruitful encounter emerged a vigorous upper-caste Vellala Tamil Christian community, into which J.C. Cornelius was born in Tanjavur in 1892. Twenty-three years younger than Gandhi, Cornelius, who changed his name to Kumarappa, was simultaneously an acolyte and a sounding board for the Mahatma. JCK studied at Madras Christian College, a leading Protestant missionary institution in south India.

At the age of twenty, JCK went to London, where he did not follow the usual upper-caste, upper-class Indian path. Instead of studying law, JCK decided to study the very practical discipline of accounting and became one of the new-fangled tribe of qualified and certified 'chartered accountants'. JCK returned to Bombay in India and set up an accounting firm. The lure of academia never went away from him. In 1926, while on holiday in New York, at the relatively late age of thirty-four, JCK enrolled as a student at Syracuse University. Again, he chose the very practical discipline of business administration. He subsequently moved to Columbia University, where he had his tryst with the dismal science. Kumarappa obtained a master's degree in economics from Columbia. His dissertation was entitled 'The Contribution of Public Finance to the Present Economic State of India'. Kumarappa returned to India and first met the Mahatma in 1929. Gandhi was instantly taken by Kumarappa. He favoured and honoured JCK by serializing his Columbia thesis in his own journal *Young India*, where its title was shortened in an appropriately incendiary manner into 'Public Finance and Our Poverty' (Redkar, 2019).

Christian Pietism in the Background

Before we discuss Kumarappa's engagement with Gandhi's intellectual evolution, it is worth getting back to the Christian Pietist connection, as it has a bearing on Gandhi's actions even prior to his meeting with JCK. There appears a strange serendipity in the parallel excursions of the Mahatma and the Pietists. Ziegenblag was a disciple of the German Christian thinker August Hermann Francke. Francke's patron, Prince Friedrich of Brandenburg in Germany, had funded a university in a town called Halle as early as in the late 1600s. 'From 1695, Francke created at Halle an extraordinary complex of orphanage, medical clinic, schools for both poor children and young noblemen and a teacher-training college complete with printing press, library . . .' (MacCulloch, 2010). This could very well be a description of any one of the settlements/farms/ashrams that Gandhi established. Count Zinzendorf, who was of the earlier-mentioned Moravian Christian Pietist connection, also undertook a project to build a showcase village named Hernhut, 'a place for craftwork and farming' (MacCulloch, 2010). The community platforms required to develop human capital in eighteenth-century Germany in a Christian ambience, or in twentieth-century South Africa or India in a multi-faith atmosphere, seem to be strikingly similar!

Education as a Community Experience

Marjorie Sykes, a talented and idealistic Englishwoman who worked with Gandhi, has noted the fact that the community itself was in some sense a school from the Gandhian perspective (Sykes, 2009). Practical problems remained. His involvement in setting up and organizing pioneering communities forced Gandhi to take a formal interest in education. In Durban and in Johannesburg, he gathered many of his political followers, and they started living together in groups at Phoenix Settlement and at Tolstoy Farm. Whole families came together to live in these places. And with the families came children who did not have access to established schools. Instead of treating this matter as a minor issue, Gandhi decided to make education a central concern in his settlements/farms/ashrams. There arose an extraordinary opportunity for Gandhi to experiment. Experimentation was in any event dear to his heart, which is perhaps why he referred to his autobiography as *The Story of My Experiments with Truth*. By the 1930s, Gandhi had learned enough from his experiments, his readings and his contacts, to boldly set forth his vision of an ideal New Learning system, which was implicitly his recommendation for India, which clearly was not very far from political freedom.

It is not as if Gandhi's efforts in the field of education were entirely sui generis. Other public figures like Madan Mohan Malaviya and Sir Syed Ahmed Khan had set up universities at Benares and Aligarh.

Gandhi's approach, though, was different in that his focus was largely on primary, pre-teen and early-teen education. Additionally, he viewed this education as part of the overall experiment of community living, either in his ashrams or in the idealized village of his imagination. The idea of 'sending' children far from their living quarters to a distant and distinct institution called a school is something that seems to have never occurred to the Mahatma. The educational experiment, like all his other activities, had to be tied up with the overarching political objective of the Indian national freedom movement—independence from the baneful influences of the British empire. Gandhi and his Nai Talim or New Learning approach would be an authentically Indian offering, which, like so many of the Mahatma's endeavours, would always have a universalist flavour.

Nai Talim's Rejection of Alternative English Models

It is interesting to note that Gandhi's proposal for school education was completely at odds with the efforts of other members of the Indian elite, who, for example, set up an all-boys boarding school known as the Doon School, almost entirely on the lines of an English boarding school. Such a school was very far indeed from Gandhi's ideals and ideas. Ashis Nandy has pointed out that almost everything in Gandhi's thought process represented a rejection of the hyper-masculine bullying penumbra that surrounded English boarding schools (Nandy, 2009). It is interesting to note that Gandhi's disciple Jawaharlal Nehru, himself an English boarding school product, had his grandchildren attend the elite all-boys Doon School. As we will subsequently examine, it is almost certainly on account of this foundational difference in weltanschauungs between Gandhi and other sections of the Indian elite that Gandhi's Nai Talim was abandoned by independent India, even while it continued to render theoretical obeisance to the Mahatma.

Nai Talim or New Learning can be viewed as a pedagogical doctrine that combined the visions of Gandhi, Montessori and J.C. Kumarappa. Nai Talim was referred to in English as Basic Education. Perhaps this English rendering was unfortunate. It gave the impression of being something rudimentary and primitive. It was therefore appropriate for poor villagers and not suited for elite children, who would naturally and obviously gravitate to the Doon School model. It is also the case that many of the proponents of Nai Talim, including Kumarappa, over-emphasized their desire to take Nai Talim to the villages. This resulted in crucial pedagogical doctrines like 'tinkering' not getting the attention they deserved. Villages, after all, were viewed with a combination of disdain and horror by the likes of Nehru and Ambedkar, and in early twentieth-century India the very mention of 'village' invoked images of backwardness in the minds of these intellectuals. In this, they were one with Marx and Engels, whose reference to 'rural idiocy' has acquired legendary status (Marx and Engels, 2002).

It is important to strip away from Nai Talim several associated ideas which may not even have been central to its conceptualization. This will enable us to evaluate the system on its own terms and to even understand its contemporary relevance in human capital development. In 1945, Kumarappa published his extraordinary volume *Economy of Permanence*. Gandhi wrote a foreword to the book, and while recommending it to readers he warned them the book was not as easy to understand as Kumarappa's earlier work. 'It needs careful reading twice or thrice if it is to be fully appreciated.' Many of Kumarappa's ideas may appear quaint or outdated to the contemporary reader. But such a reading would be uncharitable. It is important to set the book in the context of a country struggling to regain freedom after being wounded for many years. Such a situation leads to a natural level of hyperbole. It is equally important that, like Gandhi, Kumarappa was deeply concerned with religion and spirituality. The mystical exaggerations in Kumarappa's prose can be attributed to this. The contemporary sceptical reader needs to approach Kumarappa's text with empathy and respect rather than with the purpose of making summary condemnations.

Kumarappa's Nai Talim Manifesto

Here are some selected quotes from Kumarappa's book as he introduces Nai Talim or Basic Education or the Wardha Scheme (as the tenets were first articulated in Wardha, where Gandhi had set up yet another ashram):

> [The proposal] recommends a course of seven years' compulsory basic education for boys and girls from the age of seven to fourteen. The medium of instruction is to be a craft like spinning around which all subjects are taught. The everyday life of the child and the correlation of the craft, the physical and social environment of the child afford points of coordination for all departments of knowledge.

Except for the reference to spinning, this could come out as a text by any Montessori expert. The idea that a craft could be a medium of instruction is breathtakingly powerful, and any education guru who misses that thought loses much. Kumarappa goes on to further heights of brilliance.

> There will be no effort to teach writing until the child has learnt drawing. Reading will be taught first. After the age of twelve, the pupil may be allowed to choose a craft as a vocation . . . when intellectual training comes first, we, in a way tie the hands and feet of the child and he becomes impractical . . . Instruction without experience becomes a pure memory training exercise. It does not develop any initiative or personality . . . The brunt of the examinations will be borne by the teaching staff not by pupils under this scheme (Kumarappa, 2010).

A simple content analysis of these quotations can be quite stimulating. There is a complete sense of gender equality in the approach, not something that was very obvious or fashionable seventy-five years ago. Then there is the issue of the agency of the child. It is important to note that a twelve-year old child is not forced but given the opportunity to choose carpentry or smithy or weaving as a craft. The child is not forced to opt for something where aptitude and liking are absent. There is a rejection of rote learning and the dreaded prospects of examinations are banished from the child's mind. Kumarappa was probably thinking about Gandhi's terrifying examination experience in his Porbandar school when the future Mahatma mis-spelled the word 'kettle' in the august presence of a visiting British examiner!

Nai Talim has had its share of critics. Its inherent craft orientation was supposed to be inimical to 'advanced studies' in all fields, which was the forte of the great universities of the West. The best argument against this comes from Kumarappa himself. In his 1949 work, *The Philosophy of Work and Other Essays*, JCK emerges as an eloquent Francis Bacon in his defence of the organic connection between abstract knowledge and practical applications. He has this to say: 'No one can become a great musician, just by listening to good music; hours and hours of practice is necessary. Similarly, a good scientist cannot become a scientist unless he spends hours in a laboratory, labouring hard with new experiments and bearing the odour of sulphuretted hydrogen.' Clearly, there is no reason to believe that Nai Talim could not or would not accommodate the pursuits of physics, chemistry or music. The only point to note is that there would be a great deal of emphasis on practice, on laboratory work. Gandhi's favourite activity of gardening turns out to have been a favourite of the redoubtable Francis Bacon too. Bacon wrote: 'Gardening is the noblest of human professions.' In recent times, this approach may actually help better in teaching the now fashionable subject of 'environmental science' in a direct manner rather than through a dull textbook methodology.

Both Gandhi and Kumarappa were able to glide easily from music and the sciences to engineering and agricultural studies. Gandhi's statement of 1936 is along the lines one would expect from the sensitive votary of Indian human capital development that he was: 'When Americans come and ask me what service they could render, I tell them, if you dangle your millions before us, you will make beggars of us, and demoralize us. But in one thing I don't mind being a beggar. You can ask your engineers and agricultural experts to place their services at our disposal.' At one stroke, Gandhi makes the points that misplaced charity can be morally corrosive for the recipient, that agency for India's economic growth rests with Indians and that educational expertise is welcome from all parts of the world. American engineers and agricultural scientists will receive red-carpet treatment, as did the Italian pedagogical expert Maria Montessori and the Polish Jewish engineer Frydman.

The second criticism is that the craft-based approach did not give enough importance to the pursuit of arts. Kumarappa's insistence that drawing lessons should precede writing lessons should by itself take care of this argument. Nai Talim also gave a great deal of emphasis to music and dramatics. It is a pity that Kumarappa uses expressions like 'folk music' and makes references to 'village festivals'. This results in many uncharitable critics going back to the view that Nai Talim was something primitive and unsophisticated. In retrospect, one wishes that the primers on Nai Talim had simply mentioned music and drama. Kumarappa's references to bhajan, kirtan and important religious occasions as important community activities that had relevance to Nai Talim may also raise concerns in some quarters. Kumarappa's own words are the best counter: 'No nation can ever hope to take its place in the vanguard of the nations which has not got its roots in its own culture. We cannot shine on borrowed feathers. We have to develop our own contribution to the world of literature, art and music.' Despite or because he was born into a devout Christian family, Kumarappa spent his life establishing an Indian—even a Hindu—identity, as suggested by his need to change his name. He saw nothing narrow-minded or improper in acknowledging his country's culture just the way it was, rather than raising objections about exclusivist mono-culturalism, as is the habit of many contemporary academics.

Another criticism of Nai Talim is that it has little or no focus on collegiate and other higher-education issues. Gandhi would have pleaded guilty. He said with emphasis: 'I attach the greatest importance to primary education . . .' However, neither the Mahatma nor Kumarappa were entirely indifferent to the challenges associated with the development of higher education in India. Kumarappa's views on the financing of technical colleges are worth paying attention to. 'Of course, as Gandhi suggested, college education must be made self-supporting. An agricultural college which cannot maintain itself on the land allotted to it belies the object for which it exists. Similarly, all other professional and technical colleges should be made to pay for themselves.'

Kumarappa was conscious that the craft items produced by schoolchildren would not be sufficient to cover all the costs of the school. He nevertheless believed that even partial self-financing was desirable. Nai Talim's repetitive concerns with financial viability seem to have arisen from the importance attached to community autonomy and the fear of remote control by an uncaring state. Gandhi and Kumarappa seem to have anticipated Raghuram Rajan's concern about the neglect of the energies present in neighbourhood communities when public policy gets concerned only with the mighty market or the mightier state (Rajan, 2019). Kumarappa's suggestion apropos of college finance also has an interesting connotation. It seems to anticipate the current fashion among universities around the world, of treating their discoveries and inventions as potential revenue streams around intellectual property. Whether one agrees with this approach entirely or not, credit should be given to Kumarappa for envisaging this possibility as early as in the 1940s. The importance of revenue streams for sustaining like-minded communities and educational ventures under them has a Christian

Pietist connection also. While setting up his establishment in Halle, which has been referred to earlier, the redoubtable August Francke was involved with the 'first commercial production in Europe of standardized medical remedies' (MacCulloch, 2010). Perhaps the subliminal Pietist influence was at the root of Kumarappa's thought process.

Gandhi's overarching insistence on clean surroundings, proper sanitation and civic hygiene were incorporated into the Nai Talim curriculum as a matter of course. It seemed natural to both Gandhi and Kumarappa that children should be actively encouraged to sweep their classrooms, collect garbage and where possible convert bio-garbage into manure, and so on. This programme did not draw explicit criticism, but it did succeed in making many wary of the contours of Nai Talim. It is pertinent to wonder whether persons who are reasonably highly educated in independent India's education system and who routinely litter streets, highways and picnic spots may not have emerged as more responsible citizens if they had done a little bit of sweeping and cleaning in their school days under a Nai Talim regime.

Another, almost extraneous concern arose not from Nai Talim per se, but from the positions that Gandhi and Kumarappa took on the age-old Indian question of caste. Both believed that caste in the days of antiquity was a sensible system of division of labour in society. Theorists of this school routinely ascribed the dysfunctional nature of caste in the twentieth century to the so-called 'distortions' which arguably had crept in over time. Kumarappa angered his critics even more by peppering his classic book *Economy of Permanence* with pretty eccentric comments that favoured Brahmins and Kshatriyas, derided Banias and patronized Sudras. By the standards of the twenty-first century, these statements may be outlandish. But it is safe to wager that the underlying argument about an idealized caste system in the distant past and its subsequent degeneration will remain with us almost forever, either on the surface or in a subterranean way, in a manner described in a different context by Amartya Sen (2005).

As Chaitra Redkar describes it, Kumarappa was nothing if not a high-caste Vellala. While his intellectual integrity is not in doubt, his origins probably do have bearing on his views. But it needs to be emphasized that his arguments on caste are not at all related to his positions on Nai Talim. Both Gandhi and Kumarappa were emphatic that children of all castes must participate together in the Nai Talim programme, which tolerated no discrimination on the basis of caste, religion or gender.

Language too became a source of controversy associated with Nai Talim. Gandhi and Kumarappa were implacably opposed to the excessive use of English, for obvious political reasons. But given the number of languages in India and the political associations around these languages, a measure of confusion and controversy was inevitable. The Muslim League saw the emphasis on Hindi as an attack on Urdu and the Muslim identity. Many south Indians were supporters of English usage because they felt English was their best defence against what they feared was a subtle and inexorable attempt to impose Hindi on them. These criticisms could have been easily addressed if Gandhi and Kumarappa had been more sensitive to their opponents and less determined in their distaste for English. Given that the proposed medium of instruction was spinning, and given that writing was planned to be taught well after drawing was learned, the language controversy could easily have been dealt with. But that did not happen, and the opponents of Nai Talim found a useful weapon. There is, however, every reason to believe that once Independence had been achieved and the political rationale for opposing the English language had disappeared, Nai Talim could and would have accommodated and welcomed the teaching and learning of English. It must not be forgotten that Gandhi had an amazing mastery over the English language. The Mahatma seemed to have known by heart entire passages from the King James English Bible. He could also quote extensively and effortlessly from Shakespeare. Parel points this out in his foreword to the Mahatma's famous Allahabad 1916 speech. Kumarappa too was no novice when it came to use of the English language. In 1949, Kumarappa published a book which had an evocative title: *Stone Walls and Iron Bars*. It takes a truly intimate knowledge of English poetry to be able to use as a title the eloquent lines from the poem 'To Althea from Prison', by the poet Richard Lovelace. The full quotation reads as follows: 'Stone walls do not a prison make, Nor iron bars a cage.' It stands to reason that after Indian independence, neither Gandhi's soul nor the living Kumarappa, who was alive till 1960, would have had any problems in incorporating English into the Nai Talim programme.

The Boarding School Contrast

One needs to contrast Kumarappa's school (allowing for the fact that the very expression 'school' needs to be loosely used in this context) with St Cyprians, an all-boys English boarding school attended by George Orwell some hundred years ago. The exercise in comparative analysis is relevant, because India's post-Independence elites consciously chose to patronize Indian versions of St Cyprians. According to Orwell, apart from being an unhappy, brutal, sadistic place, his school had only one goal for poorer children like him: success in scholarship examinations. The richer and well-connected children did not even have to pursue this goal. They could confine themselves to hearty bullying and violent football. Here are some rather extensive quotations from Orwell:

'. . . The greatest outrage of all was the teaching of history . . .' ;
    'They were the kind of stupid question that is answered by rapping out a name or a quotation.';
    Who plundered the Begams? Who was beheaded in an open boat?';
    'Almost all our historical teaching was on this level.'

One of Orwell's teachers was a particularly cruel lady whose nickname was Flip. She terrified the boys with questions regarding important dates from history. She would read out the date, and from memory the boys had to spit out the name of the associated event. And God help the boys who got the answer wrong. "'1587?" "Massacre of St. Bartholomew!" "1707?" "Death of Aurangzeb!" "1713?" "Treaty of Utrecht!" . . . "1520?" "Oo, Mum, please Mum".' It is the height of irony that the schooling systems of independent India imitated Orwell's pre-World War I English boarding school. Corelli Barnett would have rued the fact that independent India stayed with the theoretical and academic emphasis that characterized the British Indian education system. It is perhaps uncharitable to note that Orwell mentions that corporal punishment was never meted out to rich boys. Jawaharlal Nehru, being a rich boy, perhaps had a more enjoyable time in his English boarding school, and this might have influenced his preferences (Orwell, 2000).

The Alternative Scottish Enlightenment Tradition

There was another European tradition of education and training more compatible with Gandhi's Nai Talim and Kumarappa's views. One can think of James Watt literally tinkering with Newcomen's steam engine, watching the steam escape, tightening a valve here and opening up a spout there—and voila! coming up with a new improved version! The rest, as they say, is history. It is important to remember that Watt the tinkerer was as central to the Scottish Enlightenment as the philosophers Adam Smith and David Hume. Watt was actually a good friend of Adam Smith. Watt was not relegated to some poor corner reserved for the lowly. Watt was made a fellow of the prestigious Royal Society of Edinburgh. Watt's education, as it turns out, seems to have been modelled after Nai Talim. At first, he was schooled at home by his mother and not 'sent' to a school. When he went to a formal school, he showed no aptitude for Greek or Latin (contrast this with poor Orwell, who was frequently beaten for making mistakes with Greek sentence construction, an activity which he hated). After school, Watt did not enter the portals of an academic university. He started working in a workshop, which has a direct connect with the German practical apprenticeship system and Kumarappa's emphasis on vocations. Watt exercised agency—in a manner that would have warmed Kumarappa's heart—and 'chose' to focus on engineering models. The story of Watt playing around with his mother's kettle (something which Kumarappa would have approved of) is generally considered an apocryphal one. But like all such stories, there may be an indirect link. Watt did actually use kettles when he was working on subjects like heat conservation and thermal losses. Watt was into tinkering in multiple ways. He acquired his skills as an instrument-maker while repairing instruments made by others. For a brief period he even made musical instruments and toys. The most important comment about Watt came from Humphry Davy, who points out that Watt's practical skills were in actual fact overshadowed by his theoretical knowledge. It perhaps goes to prove that good practice rarely comes in the way of enunciation of good theories (Lira, 2001).

Confronting Mutually Reinforcing Traditions

It is intriguing to consider whether Gandhi and Kumarappa were positing an educational pathway which would have enabled India to produce many tinkering James Watts. Gandhi was always into practical empiricism and kept his theoretical interests to a minimum. He actually prevailed upon Maurice Frydman to tinker with the traditional charkha and improve it. That entire episode is quite reminiscent of Watt improving Newcomen's engine. Indian education had in many respects inherited multiple theoretical traditions. Over the years, India's traditional Brahminical education became addicted to endless memorization and abstract disputation. Brahmins were forbidden to do manual physical labour, while blacksmiths had limited or no access to theoretical treatises on metallurgy. The connection between theory and practice became difficult, if not impossible. Ritual 'pollution' rules particularly hurt the development of disciplines like zoology and physiology, as dealing with animal carcasses and human cadavers was considered polluting by many upper-caste Hindus. When the British scholastic education system was introduced into India, the emphasis remained on theory and on examination success. This conjunction of two mutually reinforcing philosophies of education was extremely inimical to tinkering as a learning methodology. This, of course, considerably reduced the probability of the emergence of a James Watt in India—little wonder that it took a Polish Jew to make a better charkha for India!

There were always exceptions and workarounds in India where traditions were concerned. Stories of the legendary Susruta stealing corpses in Benares in order to study them are part of an enduring mythology. In British India, Jagdish Chandra Bose, Prafulla Chandra Ray and C.V. Raman, all emerged as experimental scientists of eminence. Viswesvarayya emerged as an engineer who enjoyed working long hours in a smelting plant. But these examples are just too few, especially when you compare them with the galaxy of lawyers and civil servants that the British Raj brought forth. It must not be forgotten that Raman faced considerable pressure to be a pen-pushing civil servant rather than a physicist immersed in his laboratory. The mathematician Ramanujan faced immense difficulties because he could not cram and pass examinations in subjects in which he had no interest. Nai Talim can and should be seen as a way out of the logjam that could result in many more exceptions surfacing. The intriguing question is whether even a partial adoption of Nai Talim in independent India might not have changed the direction of our human capital development and impacted our growth trajectory.

Tinkering and Its Absence

Independent India chose an education system which was completely at odds with Nai Talim. Rigid classroom disciplines, memorization, rote learning and no emphasis on physicality or motor skills in the Montessori mode—in short, they offered no tinkering opportunities for children. The focus on theoretical knowledge and a rigid written examination and certification system resulted in minimal or no acquaintance with physical manual labour. Tossed away were Gandhi's concerns about restoring a sense of dignity to manual work and thereby digging at the foundations of caste identities. But the singular achievement of independent India's education system seems to have been that it precluded the emergence of someone like the Scotsman Watt or the American genius Thomas Edison, who too was a product of home-schooling, indifferent formal schooling, no university exposure and hands-on apprenticeship of the tinkering variety. The career of Edison has led to the emergence of the enduring myth of American garage tinkerers. Gandhi's favourite Fredrick Singer too clearly falls in this category.

Both Edison and Singer became enormously successful and wealthy. The former is considered a national icon. The contrast with G.D. Naidu, who was sometimes referred to as India's Edison, is noteworthy. Naidu hated school and was a tinkerer who taught himself a great deal about automobiles and machines. He successfully ran a bus transport company, which the state in independent India nationalized. He designed a two-seater petrol engine car as early as in 1952. The car cost a mere two thousand rupees. But Naidu was forced to shut down his plant. He was denied the much sought after 'license' to manufacture cars. Licenses were tightly controlled by the government and given only to the favoured few (Satyamurty, 2009). This shows that the dislike of persons who tinkered extended beyond the field of education in India. It impacted businesses considerably, and almost always negatively.

Modern Indian Education: Attempts and Patterns

It is important to maintain a balanced view of the education system in British India and in independent India. Barnett's view that it was not only about literature, history and law is more than a tad unfair. As early as in 1871, a college was established in England with the specific objective of training British engineers for work in India. The idea of providing such opportunities to Indians was slower in coming, but it did eventually arrive. Engineering institutions at Poona, Roorkee, Madras and Dhanbad surely began to make their presence felt alongside the law colleges of Bombay, Calcutta and Madras. But even as these marginal efforts were made, the colonial education system remained a prisoner to rigid academic orthodoxy (Subramanian, 2020). The redoubtable G.D. Naidu, as principal of the Government College of Technology in Coimbatore, came to the conclusion that a four-year study programme was unnecessary and costly and that a two-year one would suffice if supplemented with practical apprenticeships. Naidu's efforts at change were stymied and he had to resign his post (Satyamurty, 2009). Nehru, with his strong attachment to science and technology, went out of his way to create the ecosystem of the Indian Institutes of Technology. But even this effort remained selective and elitist, as independent India continued to adhere to the education policies of the Raj (Subramanian, 2020). The first three decades of independent India were marked by an acute 'shortage' of places in engineering colleges, making the dreaded entrance examinations central events in the lives of youngsters belonging to the emerging middle class.

Fearing that easy establishment of educational institutions could lead to dangerous seditious tendencies, the British had insisted that universities and colleges could only be set up with government approval, and their actual administration was closely monitored by government officials. This top-down approach to education continued in independent India. Colleges needed state approval for the number of students they could admit. This resulted in a self-induced shortage in educational requirements. This approach would have been completely unacceptable to Gandhi and Kumarappa. In JCK's words: 'Centralization of education, as in other spheres, leads to too much control from those at a distance. Centralization of education will lead to hide-bound methods and standardization which are fatal to true education' (Kumarappa, 2010). Luckily, the much-maligned Indian tradition of corruption found an unlikely solution to the problem of shortage of places in educational institutions. Politicians in the southern Indian states were the first to realize that there was money to be made in engineering education, as parents were willing to pay substantial fees to help their children along. State governments became generous in granting approvals to their friends and benefactors who went on to set up literally hundreds of engineering colleges as this phenomenon spread to numerous states. It could be argued that India's emergence as a major producer of computer software is directly the result of the human capital created by this plethora of engineering colleges. The elitist criticism of the so-called poor quality of these institutions misses the point. When it comes to human capital, numbers matter. The larger the available workforce the better. And if the denominator is large, sufficient numbers of high-quality persons will emerge.

Many reasons can be found for India's relative success in the field of information technology and its glaring failure in manufacturing. While problems associated with land availability, poor infrastructure, rigid labour laws, inordinate regulatory burdens, inadequate power and transport situations are all frequently publicized, and perhaps rightly so, one might wish to look at the absence of the tinkering tradition in our human capital development. Engineering education has been rendered into a theoretical, white-collar, air-conditioned-office affair. The connections with the shop floor, the foundry and the proverbial garage were minimized by the so-called prescribed syllabus of the acronym- and abbreviation-oriented bureaucratic system, so detested by the Mahatma and JCK. The government set up the august-sounding University Grants Commission (UGC) and the All India Council of Technical Education (AICTE), which presumably is more august in so far as there are more letters to reckon with. By their very constructs, they had to be opponents of tinkering creativity and laissez faire learning—for such activities cannot be centrally examined and graded.

To be fair, both the Central and state governments did attempt to set up Polytechnics and Industrial Training Institutes, which were presumably less theoretical and closer to the factory floor. But the octopus of academic officialdom inherited from the British went into caricature mode when these institutions were put under the control of the extra august-sounding Directorate of Technical Education (DTE), which was safely and cosily ensconced in an air-conditioned office in the state capital and whose suffocating controls ensured that there was in fact no scope for tinkering and limited or minimal interaction between these institutes and real-life factories. Tinkering skills in the aggregate can result in improved and more efficient manufacturing. They may also result in achievements in product design. As on date, Brazilian-designed and manufactured civilian aircraft are available. Despite having large numbers of theoretically qualified engineers, India lags behind Brazil in aeronautical engineering. The fact that computer science is the most coveted subject in Indian engineering colleges and that mechanical engineering and aeronautical design are looked down upon may have something to do with it. Once again, we have the repeat motif of disdain for tinkering and a continued adulation for the textbook and the keyboard!

Towards a Resolution: Tinkering Gandhi as a Human Capital Guru

Tinkering as an educational methodology which leads to creativity, innovation and economic success is not just about historical snippets. Its contemporary relevance is quite astonishing. Hewlett and Packard are still admired for their work in their garage and are almost seen as the fathers of the now-famed Silicon Valley in California. This, by all accounts, has encouraged many others to choose garages and abandoned warehouses from where to launch their ventures. The college dropout Steve Jobs turns out to be the tinkerer par excellence. He was obsessively concerned with the physical contours of his products and how they behaved in the context of eye-hand coordination and responses to fingers. Jobs would perhaps have understood Gandhi's quasi-mystical interest in the charkha. He would have also in all likelihood reacted very favourably to Kumarappa's version of craft mysticism: '. . . the life and thought of the consumer is closely entwined with the life and the creative faculty of the producer'. In turn, Gandhi would have approved of Jobs's interest in calligraphy. Gandhi was ashamed of his poor handwriting and would have reacted well to the idea that training in calligraphy (a lot of eye-hand-finger coordination there) would have helped him write more legibly and attractively.

It is not necessary to make the case that the English boarding school system is all bad, if after all it could produce an Orwell and a Robert Graves who, like Orwell, was an unrelenting critic of his boarding school and all that it represented (Graves, 2014). The emphasis on sports need not be laughed at merely because Orwell and Graves had strong views on the subject. Similarly, the liberal education provided by universities like Oxford and Cambridge and their imitators in India need not be subject to caricature a la Corelli Barnett. With all its faults, the post-Independence Indian education system has also performed well in many respects. The energy, the willingness to work long hours, the let-me-do-my-homework-or-mother-will-be-upset syndrome that characterizes the student group in India's emerging middle class, which includes many from the lowest castes, the effortless mastery of painstaking computer programming—these are features that should not be arrogantly dismissed.

To look for an 'either-or' resolution is in all probability not going to be fruitful. The appropriate way forward may be to agree that elements of Nai Talim, particularly its focus on hands-on tinkering, can add to and improve our school education system. To start with, spinning, carpentry, smithy, weaving and gardening can be included as important subjects in our school curriculum. It is vital that these disciplines not be accorded the status of 'optional' stuff, whose marks and grades don't count. That is the surest way to ensure that they are ignored. More importantly, if the idea that 'tinkering' has a disproportionate positive impact is drilled into students, parents, teachers and the public at large, it may very well turn out that in a few decades, several desirable consequences emerge. The Atal Tinkering Laboratories introduced in many schools by the Indian government can be seen as a belated recognition of Gandhi's ideas. It is important that these laboratories do not become purely computer coding shops where the only physical activity consists of usage of the keyboard. Activities like hands-on metal bending should receive equal importance. Then India may finally reach its constantly missed tryst with manufacturing and factories. India's human capital development may actually leverage Gandhi's ideas, even if this happens in the kind of factories that the *Hind Swaraj* did not approve of. Indians may emerge as designers and India as the design studio that makes many objects large and small that consumers around the world fall in love with. (The irony may lie in the fact that Gandhi may not have approved of these products.) Indian agriculture too may benefit in many unanticipated ways as energized students of the Nai Talim gardening syllabus go on to become tinkering graduates of agricultural colleges and improve performance in that sector. These students may also contribute to a cleaner and a more environmentally sustainable country. Indian students may end up being better educated in the holistic sense of that term. The New Education Policy of the Government of India should at a minimum acknowledge Gandhi's Nai Talim in its section on vocational education and leverage Kumarappa's ideas in the execution phase. The Mahatma may end up as an unlikely guru of our human capital development story.

11

Gandhi's Trusteeship: Perspectives and Approaches*

Gandhi's Own Words

Luckily for us, there is no dearth of material left behind by Gandhi covering his views on trusteeship. He wrote on the subject not only in the *Harijan* and in *Young India,* the publications founded by him, but also in other newspapers and magazines like the *Amrita Bazaar Patrika* and the *Modern Review.* He spoke on the subject before different audiences. He gave extensive interviews on trusteeship to

---

* In Chapter 11, I have avoided repeated use of brackets and references to CW, 1999 given the numerous direct quotations of Gandhi. The Gandhi quotations referenced in this chapter are from issues of *Harijan*, 1 June 1935, 20 February 1937, 25 June 1938, 3 June 1939, 16 December 1939, 8 June 1940, 25 August 1940, 1 February 1942, 8 March 1942, 16 February 1947, 23 February 1947 and 24 October 1948; *Reporting Talk*, 22 August 1934; *Young India*, 6 October 1927, 26 March 1931 and 26 November 1931; *Amrita Bazar Patrika*, 3 August 1934; *Modern Review*, October 1935; *Autobiography*; Lecture at the Economics Society, Muir College, Allahabad, 1916; all cited in CW, 1999. Furthermore, in Chapter 11, specific references not cited are the Gospel of St. Mark, The Gospel of St. Matthew, the Bhagavad Gita and the Isavasya Upanishad, as their quotations are frequently embedded in Gandhi's quotes.

a variety of interlocutors, including a long one to a certain Pierre Ceresole, the president of the International Voluntary Service, an organization headquartered in Britain, which worked for international peace. From Gandhi's writings and speeches, it is not difficult to put together the fact that his sources of inspiration were English common legal traditions, Gujarati Jain and Vaishnava Bania traditions, the Isavasya Upanishad, the Bhagavad Gita and the Gospels of the New Testament, all of which he internalized and seasoned with his own direct experiences in dealing with wealthy capitalists as well as radical socialists. The net result may not have been a single comprehensive book or tome. But it is possible to put it all together and come up with an important theoretical contribution that the Mahatma has made in the realm of political economy. One can grant that it is not an entirely original theory. It does have similarities with the Quaker approach to stewardship of business activities and wealth. But it is both original and seminal in terms of the elements that Gandhi emphasizes, endorses and discards. From a moral philosophy perspective, one can establish a link in Gandhi's contribution with Adam Smith, with the Scottish Enlightenment concerns about human existence in society, with the ancient Indic intellectual engagement with the purusharthas or the goals of the good life. Surprisingly, or perhaps not so surprisingly, given the evergreen nature of many of the Mahatma's views and insights, one can establish a link with contemporary thought in the areas of identity economics and behavioural economics. The attempt in this chapter is to capture Gandhi's insights on trusteeship pretty much in his own words and to establish it as a credible theory, not to position it as a doctrine where the Mahatma speaks in an almost ex-cathedra tone with full authority, although that sometimes is the wish of his so-called followers.

Trusteeship: Ethical and Legal Perspectives

It starts with the simplest of arguments. The Isavasya Upanishad says: '. . . all that moves in the universe, is pervaded by the Lord.'

If one accepts this proposition, the very idea that wealth can belong to, or be 'owned' by an individual, is a self-evident absurdity. The individual is at best a temporary trustee. Private possession itself is not held to be impure. This position is important, as on more than one occasion Gandhi presents himself as a defender of private property and property rights. He never quite gave up either on his Bania roots or his English legal training. Even after the individual has abandoned the sense of ownership and has entered the role of trustee, Gandhi is emphatic that the 'legal ownership in the transformed condition vests in the trustee, not in the State'. So opposed is Gandhi to expropriation by the State that he goes on to say: 'It is to avoid confiscation that the doctrine of trusteeship comes into play, retaining for the society the ability of the original owner in his own right.' There is absolute clarity as far as Gandhi is concerned. The 'original' owner's property rights, prior to his becoming a trustee by his own volition, remain unchanged. This is something that implicitly benefits society. One can see echoes of Maitland and the English view that property rights not only benefit the individual property-holder, but also result in social good. Gandhi's approach to transition of trusteeship also seems to emanate from the English traditions when he talks about how a successor to a trustee should be chosen: 'Choice should be given to the original owner who becomes the first trustee, but the choice must be finalized by the State.' One can almost visualize the King's Chancellor sagely involved in the adjudication of matters associated with trustees while faithfully trying to implement the wishes of the original grantor/settlor. Maitland believed that English civic institutions and civic society were made possible because of the doctrine of trusteeship, which allowed individuals and groups to set up associative bodies without explicit state sanction. Gandhi's emphasis is on the interiority of the individual. By becoming a trustee, which also happens without any external sanction, an individual grapples with issues of purity and impurity buried deep in the interstices of his or her own mind.

Gandhi blithely contradicts himself regarding the means employed to earn wealth. His advice to moneyed men is to earn their millions '(honestly only, of course)', curiously, retaining his advocacy of honest means within parentheses. But he also says: 'I have no hesitation in endorsing the proposition that rich men, and for that matter most men, are not particular as to the way they make money.' And he goes on to put an unusual ethical proposition, which almost sounds as if he is exonerating, even encouraging, a scheme to convert ill-gotten wealth into something sinless if the wealthy person makes a donation to the Mahatma, who puts it to pure and good use! Responding to a question on the rightness of accepting donations from tainted sources, he says:

> The gift of what you assume to be ill-gotten gains cannot lessen the guilt of the exploiter. If he had kept the money for himself, that would have been an additional count against him. If instead he makes a gift of it to me from pure motives, he escapes additional sin. It is also likely that a good use of this gift may wean the exploiter from immoral means of making money. But no blame attaches to me for having accepted the gift. As the foul waters from the drains flowing into the sea partake of its purity, even so does tainted wealth become pure when put to the purest use. There is one condition, however, that we have assumed, viz., that the gift is made and accepted out of pure motives.

It is easy to characterize Gandhi's curious attitude to the means of earning wealth as cute and self-serving because it justified his own practice of accepting donations from large cross-sections of individuals. But this misses two significant arguments. Firstly, wealth for Gandhi was always something instrumental. Its value arose only from its use. And if the use were ethical, that condoned many sins and might even be a source of repentance. Secondly, and most importantly, when discussing trusteeship Gandhi was discussing the relationship between the owner (hopefully transformed into a trustee) and wealth that already exists. In these discussions, the origins of the wealth are not the core matter being commented upon. We are discussing how wealth that has already been accumulated needs to be dealt with. While talking or writing about wealth, Gandhi's primary concern is the corrosive moral impact that great wealth can have on its possessors. While the pursuit of artha is an honourable one, it can easily degenerate. 'The art of amassing riches becomes a degrading and despicable art, if it is not accompanied by the nobler art of how to spend wealth usefully.' The Mahatma is acutely conscious that the instrument can convert a virtuous person into a vicious one. 'Let not possession of wealth be synonymous with degradation, vice and profligacy.' Gandhi loved the Parable of the Prodigal Son, so poignantly narrated by Jesus in the Gospels, and was extremely interested in redemptive human behaviour. One of the finest scenes in Attenborough's Gandhi is where the Mahatma advises a Hindu who has murdered a Muslim boy in the riots to adopt a Muslim boy and bring up the boy as a Muslim. To suggest that this implies condoning of murder is a fatuous interpretation of Gandhi's words and intentions. This position of Gandhi's is akin to Mandela's extraordinary Truth and Reconciliation Programme in post-apartheid South Africa (Mondhe, 2006). It is also important to remember that in so many of his public actions, Gandhi was obsessed with the purity of means. He even called off successful political movements when they were tainted with violence (CW, 1999, v. 26, p. 177–183). So, Gandhi was by no means advocating immoral means in the accumulation of wealth. He can, on the other hand, be seen as someone who has a humane and practical approach to the management of wealth, especially if it has been acquired from acts which during certain periods were legal, but which are from today's perspective horrifyingly immoral. One can think of slave trafficking or trading in opium, which were technically legal in their time, as falling in this category. Once again, the practical idealist in the Mahatma surprises us.

The Isavasya Upanishad also takes the position that it is perfectly in order to 'enjoy' this wealth or the benefits that this wealth makes possible. Gandhi too is quite clear that such enjoyment is permitted, and he even seems to suggest that enjoyment of wealth is enjoined. Assumption of the role of trustee requires that the perception of one's ownership of this wealth and the unfettered right to its use or misuse must be 'renounced'. The trustee is encouraged to 'take what you require for your legitimate needs'. Renunciation of the idea of ownership and assumption of the mantle of trusteeship go hand in hand. And once this mantle has been assumed, one may not take from the wealth presumably for one's lavish self-indulgence. Gandhi's ideal rich men are those for whom 'it is part of their nature to spend next to nothing on themselves', who are 'stingy on themselves'. The parallel with Weber's worldly asceticism is striking. One can almost visualize sober Quakers committed to modest dress and abstemious habits. No wonder Gandhi had a great fondness for and strong associations with Quakers. Enjoyment was for Gandhi a right of the individual, which could not and should not be fettered by the state. But the individual needed to, of his own volition, exercise this right with a sense of responsibility and obligation. For Gandhi, rights and duties are inextricably linked. Duties actually come before rights. 'If, instead of insisting on rights, everyone does his duty, there will immediately be the rule of order established among mankind . . . I venture to suggest that rights that do not flow directly from duty well-performed, are not worth having. They will be usurpations, sooner discarded the better.'

It is quite clear from this, as also from other writings, that Gandhi would have opposed contemporary entitlements. Despite his fondness for the story of Shravana, who looked after his parents, which Gandhi recounts in his autobiography, over the years his ideas evolved apropos of parental duties, and he discarded notions of unquestioned obedience. 'A wretched parent, who claims obedience from his children without doing his duty by them excites nothing but contempt.' Contemporary sociologists have extensively researched whether dysfunctional children are in part the consequences of irresponsible parenting. While Gandhi is not impervious to such consequentialism, he is concerned with the 'wretched' parent who has expectations of the entitlement of obedience, but who ends up being an object of 'contempt' because of his failure to perform his duties. No right, which of course includes the right to enjoy wealth, accrues in the absence of the performance of duties. It is almost as if Gandhi repeats in his time the maxims of Tiruvalluvar, whose Tamil classic, the *Tirukkural*, remains a foundational Indic text dealing with ethics and the interplay of aram (Sanskrit: dharma; English: righteousness) with kama/*inbam* (Sanskrit: kama; English: passion) and *porul* (Sanskrit: artha; English: wealth). The translations in brackets, while simplistic, are sufficient to make the present point. Porul/artha, while linked to wealth, is also tied up with public, political action. Gandhi develops a political creed along the lines of his advice to owners of wealth to embrace the duty of trusteeship. 'All rights to be deserved and preserved come from duty well done. Thus, the very right to live accrues to us only when we do the duty of citizenship of the world.' It is not that the Mahatma disagrees with Jeffersonian ideas about the right to life as expressed in the American Declaration of Independence (1776). He is not a supporter of the state or of princes. In fact, he echoes the American Declaration of Independence when he argues that people owe no duty to a prince who fails in his duty to 'serve' his people. The prince who neglects his duties is a 'usurper', and people 'earn the right of resisting the usurpation or misrule'. What is true of the incompetent and callous prince is true of the immoral and insensitive rich man. If the rich man does not adopt the Upanishad's advice of 'renunciation', he suffers moral degradation. He remains a 'slave' of his 'riches and passions'. And to add to that, he might very easily become a slave of the radical socialists who are waiting in the wings to 'overpower' him and his kind.

Gandhi demonstrates a peculiar capacity to mine different traditions for the best in them. Ashis Nandy makes the case that Gandhi challenged the West, especially the British, to reach back into their own traditions that the emphasis on racist imperialism and hyper-masculinity had caused them to ignore (Nandy, 2009; Nandy, 2013). Despite his strong opposition to Japanese militarism, Gandhi picks up something exemplary in Japanese traditions and history. 'I am convinced that the capitalist, if he follows the Samurai of Japan, has nothing really to lose and everything to gain.' Gandhi's stated aim is to awaken capitalists 'to their sense of duty'. And here he notes: 'The history of Japan reveals many an instance of self-sacrificing capitalists.' Even his critics must find something admirable in Gandhi's ability to visualize an ideal capitalist as a cross between a self-sacrificing Samurai and an androgynous Quaker!

Trusteeship: Empirical and Practical Perspectives

While the primary thrust of trusteeship is to awaken a moral consciousness in the minds of the wealthy, a consciousness that was posited by Christ, the 'greatest economist of his time', Gandhi in his inimitable way is not oblivious of the consequential practical issues at stake.

He has some very pointed remarks to make on the issues of inheritance and inherited wealth:

> Personally, I do not believe in inherited riches. The well-to-do should educate and bring up their children so that they may learn how to be independent. The tragedy is that they do not do so. Their children do get some education, they even recite verses in praise of poverty, but they have no compunctions about helping themselves to parental wealth.

The focus is on independence and the absence of it being a tragedy for the children. Gandhi is suggesting that the consequence of parental indulgence is that children deteriorate. He says even more forcefully:

> Much of the present imbecility of the children of the wealthy will go, if the latter can but substitute the worthy ambition of

educating their children to become independent for the unworthy ambition of making them slaves of ancestral property, which kills enterprise and feeds the passions which accompany idleness and luxury.

The practical consequences of reliance on inherited wealth are many indeed: inadequate application to education, lack of independence, and succumbing to idleness. Buried quietly along with these consequences is one that has effects not only on the children of the wealthy, but also on society at large. Inheritance can 'kill enterprise'. The Mahatma was always conscious of the need for enterprise. He was certain that 'society would be poorer' if it were to 'lose the gifts of a man who knows how to accumulate wealth'. The use of the word 'gift' is not accidental. It again harks back to the Parable of Talents in the Gospels. A person's talent is a gift of the Lord and needs to be used with a full sense of the sacred responsibility. To create a society where talent is not encouraged but is suppressed, would not pass the moral smell-test of the Mahatma. Contrariwise, to waste or misuse inherited talent (or wealth) in profligate behaviour would go against the spirit of the Gospels.

There is another very practical need for advocating voluntary trusteeship on the part of the wealthy. If the wealthy do not make gestures along these lines, they run the risk of having others forcibly expropriating their wealth. Gandhi feared a 'violent and bloody revolution' that would work to dispossess the rich. In the aftermath of the Bolshevik success in Russia, many considered this a high-probability event in India. Gandhi was quite emphatic that he did not want socialists to succeed, for 'If they get power, they will resort to confiscation of property, repudiation of debts, and similar extreme methods.' Gandhi objected to all suggestions involving the State—almost invariably mentioned by him with a capital 'S'—suppressing capitalism.

'The State represents violence in a concentrated and organized form. The individual has a soul, but the State is a soulless machine, it can

*never be weaned from violence to which it owes its very existence. Hence,
I prefer the doctrine of trusteeship.* 'His opposition to socialist doctrines
and methods was explicit: 'To inflame labour against moneyed men
is to perpetuate class hatred and all the evil consequences flowing
from it. The strife is a vicious circle to be avoided at any cost. It is an
admission of weakness, a sign of an inferiority complex.'

On balance, it appears that the Mahatma was not optimistic
about convincing socialists to change their stance. His arguments
against socialism were too basic to enable a compromise position.
He felt that socialists believed in the 'essential selfishness of human
nature'. Presumably, the Mahatma was disappointed with socialists
because they held on to a determinist and materialist position. This
denied the redemptive potential in human agency, which was very
dear to the Mahatma. 'I know that the essential difference between
man and the brute is that the former can respond to the call of
the spirit in him, can rise superior to the passions that he owns in
common with the brute, and, therefore, superior to selfishness and
violence, which belongs to the brute nature and not to the immortal
spirit of man.' It was not only their lack of emphasis on the human
spirit that was a problem with the socialists. Gandhi was concerned
about the practical impact that state-imposed egalitarianism would
have on individuals and on society:

> My idea of society is that while we are born equal, meaning that
> we have the right to equal opportunity, all have not the same
> capacity. It is, in the nature of things, impossible. For instance, all
> cannot have the same height, or colour or degree of intelligence,
> etc., therefore in the nature of things, some will have the ability to
> earn more and others less. People with talents will have more and
> they will utilize their talents for this purpose . . . I would allow a
> man of intellect to earn more, I would not cramp his talent.

A better consequentialist case for not converting equality of
opportunity into equality of outcomes cannot be made by the most

ardent free market economist. Gandhi adds that it is in the practical interest of the talented persons who earn more to use their talents 'kindly' and 'exist as trustees'. Although the intentions of socialists had a plausible veneer, which deserved approbation, their methods were completely abhorrent to the Mahatma, for whom non-violence was central. Almost tongue-in-cheek, he has this to say: 'Whilst I have the greatest admiration for the self-denial and spirit of sacrifice of our Socialist friends, I have never concealed the sharp difference between their method and mine. They frankly believe in violence and all that is in its bosom. I believe in non-violence through and through.' On top of all this, he had a deep conviction that the Indian people would not go along with 'Communism of the Russian type, that is Communism which is imposed on a people'. It would be 'repugnant to India'. But despite his objections to socialism and communism, despite his rejection of the forcible expropriation of property, despite his personal dislike of their violence, he recognized the seductive appeal of these ideologues. Hence his warning to the rich: 'They who employ mercenaries to guard their wealth may find those very guardians turning on them.' Even if the wealthy discarded his moral exhortations, Gandhi was hopeful that they would adopt some version of trusteeship, if only to save their skins. 'As for the present owners of wealth, they would have to make their choice between class war and voluntarily converting themselves into trustees of their wealth.' Clearly, Gandhi was more hopeful that he could and he would influence the wealthy, while the socialists were likely to continue as his critics and his political adversaries.

Just as it was in the practical and consequential interests of the wealthy to make the gesture of trusteeship in order to protect themselves, Gandhi saw a symmetric interest that the non-wealthy sections of society have, in non-violently and persuasively encouraging the rich to move to trusteeship. He was particularly concerned about the rhetoric of socialists: '. . . they will not be able to achieve anything beyond startling the propertied class by their unrestrained language . . . if we needlessly startle them to-day, they will just organize themselves and establish Fascism in our country . . . there is a danger . . . of Fascism being established in India, and I want to save the country from it by winning the rich over and making them our friends.' And by destroying 'freedom', Fascism loses any possible justification it might try to acquire by claiming to be 'efficient'. These observations about the temptations of fascism and the problems associated with it are to be found in the 24 October 1948 edition of the *Harijan*, in a column titled 'Talk with Gandhiji', dated 22 August 1934. Nothing should surprise about the Mahatma. This near-cynical appraisal of the motivations of the rich and the prediction that they can succumb to the temptations of fascism, surely represents an extraordinary realpolitik approach to the issue. And one wonders whether he was thinking of Quakers when he argued that the rest of society should make 'friends' with capitalists!

Trusteeship is a possible solution to the ill effects of inherited wealth causing ruination to the inheritors, to the disastrous consequences that might occur with a socialist takeover as a reaction to the insensitivity of the rich, and to the equally disastrous consequences that would occur with a fascist takeover as the rich react to threats against their persons and their wealth. Deontological morality holds that an action must be judged by itself and a determination made as to whether it is right or wrong, and not by its outcomes. The Mahatma clearly has effortlessly moved from deontological morality into the realm of consequential empiricism. The sheer audacity of the man comes across as breathtaking even as we read his words so many decades after he spoke and wrote them.

Trusteeship: Creative Tensions

An interviewer named Pierre Ceresole asks the Mahatma: 'My tangible difficulty is how long one should wait in order to carry conviction to the rich man?' Here Gandhi is faced with multiple problems. The first is that despite all the arguments that trusteeship involves the moral and psychological benefit of the wealthy, despite the argument that it makes practical sense for the wealthy on many counts, how does one deal with the absence of conviction on the part of the proverbial rich man of the Gospels? For Gandhi, persuasion is the only option: 'I have to wait until I convert him to my point of view.' Besides, the means employed have to be 'pure'. 'I disagree with the Communist. With me the ultimate test is non-violence.' And then the lawyerly liberal argument comes forth: 'I have no right to assume that I am right and he is wrong.' As he otherwise puts it, in order to succeed, such a statute should not be 'imposed from above. It will have to come from below'. So how does one square the circle? Ceresole and Gandhi go back and forth on the relative levels of his wealth that the rich man should ideally transfer to a trust. The Mahatma comes up with a truly astonishing response, which could easily obtain the acceptance of Silicon Valley capitalists of today:

> If he says: 'I am prepared to keep for myself 25 per cent and to give 75 per cent to charities,' I close with the offer. For I know that 75 per cent voluntarily given is better than 100 per cent surrendered at the point of a bayonet; and by thus being satisfied with 75 percent, I render unto Caesar the things that are Caesar's . . . With non-violence as the rule, life will no doubt be a series of compromises. But it is better than an endless series of clashes.

The first point of interest is how the Mahatma keeps coming back to the Gospels again and again in different contexts. Secondly, he is quite clear that what is rendered to Caesar is a tax by any other name. He seems to anticipate the problems facing modern governments. A wealth tax will almost certainly drive the rich away to more benign tax havens. But a voluntary commitment of wealth toward philanthropy is likely to stay sticky. Alexis de Tocqueville had noted the plethora of voluntary associations that were key to the success of democracy in America (De Tocqueville, 2003). Separately, Maitland had noted that it was the English common law institution of trusteeship that made such associations possible. In many European countries, even

in the early twentieth century, any association of more than twenty-
five persons needed state consent and was viewed with suspicion
(Macfarlane, 2002). These voluntary associations were the spines on
which Anglo-American philanthropy rested. Gandhi had hit upon
the same vocabulary and framework for his voluntary non-tax tax of
75 per cent of a rich man's wealth, which ensured that the rich man's
children did not become spoilt brats but enterprising individuals,
which gave the rich man insurance against violent radicals and a
possibly rapacious state, and which lastly perhaps helped the rich
man pass through the proverbial eye of the needle! In turn, society
made sure that enterprising wealth-creators were not held back,
that they were not encouraged to ally with potential fascist dictators
in order to protect their property, and that their incentives to run
away to a tax haven were minimized. A worthwhile attempt for sure,
even if the chances of success were modest and the extent of actual
achievement limited. In any event, it certainly appears superior to
other prescriptions for dealing with the creation and management
of wealth.

In a final stab, Gandhi makes an attempt at resolving the creative
tensions at the heart of his trusteeship doctrine with an extraordinary
insight way ahead of his time, one that anticipates many of the most
recent ideas in corporate governance, corporate social responsibility,
stakeholder capitalism, and so on. Writing in 1938, when politics was
permeated by the conflict between capital and labour, the Mahatma
chooses to introduce an unusual and unexpected third element—the
consumer. He is aware that left to themselves, capital and labour
can and will make excessive demands on the common pie. Hence,
he suggests this solution: 'In fact, capital and labour will be mutual
trustees', thus ensuring that neither side is dominant. But then he
goes on to say: '. . . and both will be trustees of consumers'. As a friend
of capitalists and as one who had a brief career as a labour leader (as
noted earlier, he even led a strike of mill workers in Ahmedabad
in 1918), Gandhi seems to be quite aware that capital and labour
could collude— particularly in conditions where their market power

was strong—to the detriment of consumers. Hence the importance that both of them don the mantle of trusteeship on behalf of and as protectors of the fiduciary interests of consumers. Till now we have Gandhi's incessant appeals to the rich to move from ownership to trustee roles. Now he moves into another orbit, where he emphasizes mutuality, checks and balances, and a fever-pointed balancing of interests of multiple groups. The focus on checks and balances harks back to the Federalist Papers of the US Founding Fathers and seems to anticipate Nobel laureate Eugene Fama's views that a modern firm is a 'nexus of contracts'. Gandhi says:

> The trusteeship theory is not unilateral, and does not in the least imply superiority of the trustee. It is as I have shown, a perfectly mutual affair, and each believes that his own interest is best safeguarded, by safeguarding the interest of the other. 'May you propitiate the gods and may the gods propitiate you, and may you reach the highest good by this natural propitiation' says the Bhagavad Gita.

By now, one must expect the unexpected from the man. But what follows is extraordinarily unusual and perhaps improper for the religious Mahatma. 'There is no separate species called gods in the universe, but all who have the power of production and will work for the community using that power are gods—labourers no less than capitalists.' At one stroke, he dispenses with the need for divine dispensation. This is plain and simple a humanist call. It reminds us of Miranda in Shakespeare's *Tempest* wondering about the marvellousness of human beings. No wonder that Gandhi maintains with great emphasis that his theory of trusteeship has not only the sanction of 'religion' but also of 'philosophy'. The most agnostic of political economists can safely offer up Gandhi's doctrine as worthy of serious consideration.

There remains the objection that trusteeship is impractical. This is notwithstanding Maitland's history, which actually celebrates the history of trusteeship's success. The Mahatma deals with this issue head-on. 'I may be a bad exponent of the doctrine in which my faith is daily increasing. Trusteeship as I conceive it, has yet to prove its worth. It is an attempt to secure the best use of property for the people by competent hands.' While his humility is touching, it is his clarity that is noteworthy. Expropriation and state ownership will simply move the property into incompetent hands. Therefore, property must be left with talented, competent individuals. But that is not enough. These talented, competent people must be encouraged to make the 'best' use of the property, not its worst use, going back once more to the instrumental nature of wealth. Curiously, trusteeship is a work in progress, as it is yet to 'prove its worth'. And it is as a work in progress that Gandhian scholars need to approach trusteeship. Precisely because the Mahatma has been seen primarily as a political theorist and practitioner, his profound contribution to political economy and the psychological underpinnings of economics have not received sufficient attention. It is time we paid attention to his own estimation of the importance of 'trusteeship', which he pointedly places within inverted commas: 'My theory of "trusteeship" is no makeshift, certainly no camouflage. I am confident that it will survive all other theories.'

12

Economist Gandhi: A Guru Relevant for Today

The Limits of Technocratic Consequentialism

The most powerful arguments in favour of modern market capitalism have been made in consequentialist terms. In other words, if something does not work well, then drop it. If something works efficiently, then pursue it. Following the stagflation of the 1970s (when Western economies simultaneously experienced both high inflation and high unemployment), Margaret Thatcher in Britain and Ronald Reagan in the US argued for drastically reducing state intervention in economies, something which had been growing ever since the end of World War II. Most Thatcher and Reagan supporters used the argument that 'markets work better'. Excessive regulation and an intrusive state were seen as inimical to economic development. There was a significant absence of philosophical or ethical argument. Most of the arguments made by Thatcher, Reagan and their followers stayed in the realm of greater efficiency of markets in the economic sphere. The problem with this approach, as presciently pointed out several decades ago by the great Austrian economist Hayek, is that they miss the overarching emphasis on human liberty (Hayek, 2014), which is central to the moral justification for market capitalism. Efficiency is merely a fortunate fallout and has no inherent moral value. By stressing technocratic economism, they also invite a sense of 'uneasiness reflected in the familiar slogan "the world is not for sale"' (Tirole, 2017).

When things go wrong and the much-vaunted efficiency is not to be seen, the emperor is accused of having no clothes. If the collapse of the Berlin wall proved that socialist collectivism was a failure, then the 2008 global economic crisis brings market capitalism into question. The response to the crisis has also been primarily technocratic: new regulations, increased supervision, more state agencies, and so on. Critics have used morally charged vocabulary in describing the crisis and its aftermath: greed, egregious greed, selfishness, insensitivity to common folk, arrogance, immorality— these are the words frequently bandied about when they refer to the economic crisis. A merely technocratic response hardly seems adequate in these circumstances. Adam Smith, for sure, would not have approved of this position. At a minimum, he would have noted the fact that the actors involved in different aspects of the 2008 crisis need to answer to their own impartial spectators. They were not atomistic individuals, but persons who actively lived in society. To protect their positions irrespective of the wider social impact would have been the behaviour of monopolists or devious merchants, who go together to ensure private interests got priority over the public weal. Such people were not Smith's heroes. Smith would have argued for a tryst with the free and responsible individual (Smith, 1982; Smith, 2002).

It is precisely the lack of moral passion and the crafting of limited technocratic responses to crises, as happened in 2008, that can be countered by revisiting the Mahatma, and hence his relevance today. It is not that Gandhi did not pay attention to practical empirical consequences. He was too shrewd a Bania and too pedantic a lawyer to ignore that aspect. His primary focus was not on action by State agencies, which he anyway distrusted. He went back to the individual, who always remained central for him. Is there a direct appeal to the individual—to her higher ethical self and to her more practical self—that can restore some of the shine that capitalism has lost? I would suggest that in examining Gandhi's words and life, we can and we will find directions, if not complete answers.

The Centrality of Trust

The word 'trust' precedes the words 'trustee' or 'trusteeship'. Nobel laureate Jean Tirole states that 'Trust is at the heart of economic and social life', and notes that the markets demand from its participants 'a significant capacity to establish trust' (Tirole, 2017). When we live in a community, which was a given for Adam Smith, when we are interconnected members of an ever-widening circle of ashrams, which was the way Gandhi viewed the world, 'trust' is an axiomatic requirement. It has legal, moral, political and practical dimensions. Specifically, in legal parlance, the grantor or settlor has confidence in the ethical, and one might add competent, behaviour of the trustee. In moral terms, the grantor/settlor actually expects the trustee to act above and beyond her self-interest. The trustee is not the familiar figure in the *Wealth of Nations* who serves a larger interest unintentionally, while she consciously pursues her own self-interest (Smith, 2002). In fact, at the heart of the construct of the trust is the view that the trustee is imbued with unselfishness. 'Nothing is more corrosive of trust than pure selfishness.' (Tirole 2017). The other moral dimension attached to the trust is that its creation has to be a voluntary act. A tax may and can be levied by a sovereign or even by a community by force. A trust cannot be so extracted.

Smith was convinced that sectional interests would capture the state. If this should happen, then actions of expropriation by the state would invariably benefit sections rather than whole communities. Gandhi distrusted the state, which he felt would oppress, deny citizens their liberties and also curb individual initiative, which for him lay at the root of human progress. For Maitland, de Tocqueville, and in recent times for the historian Francis Fukuyama, the voluntary nature of trusts, which do not require state sanction in order to be set up, has had a significant impact in the development of associative and participatory democratic organizations in countries with Anglo-Saxon common law traditions (Maitland, 2011; De Tocqueville, 2003; Fukuyama, 1995). Gandhi certainly exploited this when he set up trusts and associations, both in South Africa and India, definitely without prior state approval and in many cases just in order to fight state oppression. But for Gandhi, the voluntary nature of the trust had other moral connotations also. It fitted in both with his respect for property rights and his resolute opposition to the violence inherent in confiscatory actions. For Fukuyama, heightened trust in societies is a positive, because it enhances prospects of economic growth (Fukuyama, 1995). For Gandhi, trust was a moral imperative and voluntary trusteeship was to be commended as intrinsically desirable. That it incidentally might lead to better economic growth or to improved prospects for democratic liberty was an added positive.

One wonders as to how Gandhi would have reacted if he were told that issues concerning trust are today part of studies in experimental neuroscience. V.S. Ramachandran points out that the human brain has neurons, which get empathetically activated. If we see another person being hurt, these neurons in our brain act in a manner reflecting our empathy for the other person. As an aside, Ramachandran refers to these neurons as 'Gandhi neurons' (Ramachandran, 2011). Oddly enough, it seems that a potential trustee is biologically programmed to address her own self-interest by feeling empathy for the beneficiary of the trust. The old man might have chuckled and told us that he was right all along—humans are not mere brutes, but beings touched by the divine! He might actually not have been upset even with the experimental games conducted by Ernst Fehr, Michael Kosfeld and others, where they demonstrated that injecting a player with the hormone oxytocin increases her feeling of trust in the other player (Tirole, 2017). He, after all, held a somewhat quixotically holistic view of the human being, and he would have argued that a person's diet, eating patterns, including fasting patterns, sexual activity, or lack thereof, all interacted together to produce her thought processes and actions. However, whether he would have supported the use of a hormonal drug in order to nudge persons towards more trusting behaviour is doubtful. Whatever his response may have been, we have the freedom and opportunity to leverage Gandhi neurons and to move forward the nudge-needle, so to speak. In any event, we can at least address the oft-repeated argument that untrammelled selfishness is so innate and unchanging a part of our deep biological selves that using Gandhi's so-called impractical ideas is a tall task at best and a foolish one at worst. A friend has pointed out that this approach to understanding political economy through the lens of neuroscience has interesting possibilities and is clearly an area for substantive research. We can come away with a warm glow that the neurons of empathy have been named for our favourite Mahatma!

Both Adam Smith and Gandhi were clear that seeking to do praiseworthy actions is something natural for human beings, even though attempting to seek praise per se is not the goal. The question is: are nudges in the direction of pursuing the praiseworthy in order? In the field of evolutionary biology, the idea that individual members of species send out signals is a hoary one, going back to Charles Darwin's *Origin of the Species*. The economist Thorstein Veblen coined the expression 'conspicuous consumption'—people ostentatiously showing off their wealth in an attempt to earn stature and reputation in society. This, according to Veblen, was a form of social and economic signalling (Veblen, 2017). This leads us to the question of the appropriateness of using signalling in order to nudge persons in the direction of greater trust and the trusteeship ideal. Rather than have conspicuous consumption as the signalling, can conspicuous trusteeship be converted into the correct signalling for the leisured class? How does one ensure that trusteeship does not get hijacked in a manner that debilitates the credibility of the trust factor? In structuring incentives and nudges addressed to a simple homo economicus, or to a homo incitatus rather than a homo socialis or a homo religiosus, are we heading toward a situation where 'extrinsic incentives can kill intrinsic motivation'? (Tirole, 2017). These are the kind of questions that the theoreticians and experimenters in identity economics and behavioural economics will have to contend with, if they decide to take forward the inspiring insights that the Mahatma has left behind.

The discipline of identity economics, when it enters the normative sphere, is particularly intertwined with the human desire to become praiseworthy or to seek praise. Tirole points out that psychologists of the stature of William James and Martin Seligman '. . . have emphasized that people need to see themselves in a positive light in order to motivate themselves both to engage in activities and to further their own well-being' (Tirole, 2017). In other words, approval by the impartial spectator or the still small voice within are essential ingredients for psychological health. Gandhi laid bare before the whole world his intimate experiments with himself in his incessant effort to attain psychological health as he saw it. It is doubtless true that his efforts were guided by that ancient discipline of applied psychology known as religion, or in Gandhi's views, engagement with the Lord (Guha, 2018).

Gandhi for the Wealthy

For the wealthy, Gandhi's advice was pretty much taken out of the Gospels. Wealth has a seductive appeal. And like all seductive objects, it can be corrosive. Hedonistic excesses, slavish kowtowing to wealth and the serving of Mammon exclusively can result in loss of opportunity to engage with the Kingdom of God. And one need not take this metaphor to mean engagement with organized religion. Rather, it implies an acknowledgement that human beings are more than selfish brutes, that deep within each of us there exists an element of our consciousness that needs to have communion with the sacred. And implied by the existence of this element, an umbilical cord that ties us with the sacred, is mankind's attachment to the noblest in human traditions—the Upanishads, the Gita and the Gospels. It is the complete disconnect from the sacred that might be the persistent weakness in modern capitalist doctrines. This disconnect would have suited David Hume, but may not have passed muster with Smith's English friend Edmund Burke, and certainly not with Burke's worthy successor in recent times, Roger Scruton.

Being a worldly ascetic, as envisaged by Gandhi, meant that the individual is engaged in constructive service with her fellow-humans. Just as Gandhi disapproved of retreat into monasticism, he would today disapprove of the wealthy retreating into gated communities. I quote the Mahatma's own version of the contract which the wealthy need to have with the divine: 'If God gives us power and wealth He gives us the same so that we may use them for the benefit of mankind and not for our selfish carnal purpose.' (CW, 1999, v. 40, p. 148). While denigrating the carnal, he is perfectly fine with the connect between the aesthetic and the divine. After visiting the palatial residences of the rich people of Chettinad in south India, Gandhi has this to say: 'If you give me a contract for furnishing all these palaces of Chettinad I would furnish them with one-tenth of the money but give you a much better accommodation and comfort than you enjoy today and procure for myself a certificate from the artists of India that I had furnished your houses in a much more artistic fashion than you have done' (CW, 1999, v. 40, p. 143). His surprises never seem to end!

Gandhi for the Poor

For the poor, Gandhi had a clear message—that the pursuit of a chimerical equality with the wealthy, especially by violent means, was both immoral and impractical. Writing in the 18 August 1940 issue of *Young India*, he said: 'Economic equality must never be supposed to mean possession of an equal amount of worldly goods by everyone.' The poor do have the right, nay the duty, of 'resisting usurpation or misrule' by princes. But the resistance must not take the form of 'rapine and plunder' (CW, 1999, v. 21, p. 367). Clearly, Gandhi's message to the poor had to take into account the fact that he was a political leader in an impoverished country. He could not and did not support 'grinding pauperism' of any kind. He resorts to the Parable of the Talents in the Gospels in urging the poor to work and raise themselves rather than do so by plundering the wealthy. In contemporary terms, he would have opposed welfare dependency for the corrosion it would cause to the moral fibre of the poor. There is a Victorian Smilesian flavour to the ideas of education and hard work, which were the Mahatma's normative prescriptions. But the poor too need to live in harmony with God's edicts. If the poor were to say, '"Since we cannot all become rich and own palaces, let us at least pull down the palaces of the rich and bring them down to our level." That could bring no happiness or peace either to themselves or anyone else, and God would certainly be not the friend and helper of the poor of such description' (CW, 1999, v. 91, p. 279).

Gandhi for Business Relationships

For the complex relationship between owners and managers, Tirole makes the point that contracts and incentives, while necessary conditions, may not be sufficient. Between the principal and the agent, '. . . a relation of trust may helpfully replace formal incentives and actually improve on them' (Tirole, 2017). In the extended business world, trust emerges as a key factor. The business leader and historian of modern India, Prakash Tandon, has explored the importance of trusted relationships between companies, dealers, suppliers and agents (Rao, 2014). Gandhi's favoured model is a fallback on the Anandji Kalyanji Pedhi in his native Gujarat, where the managers are trustees for the Lord, who is the owner. This model builds on the English legal concept of trustees acting for the welfare of select beneficiaries or for large numbers of present and future beneficiaries in associative groups. The Lord as the beneficiary has the added advantage of making possible the creation of ecological environmental trusts for the benefit of future generations, who doubtless need the Lord's blessings. 'When an individual has more than his proportionate portion, he becomes a trustee of that portion for God's people. If this truth is imbibed by people generally, it would become legalized and trusteeship would become a legalized institution.' The Mahatma could not resist the temptation of being a patriotic Indian. He wished for it to become 'a gift from India to the world' (CW, 1999, v. 93, p. 355).

The emergence of businesses based on leveraging data and data analytics has introduced a whole new way to look upon trust and trusteeship. It can be argued that a firm does not 'own' its customers' data. The firm is merely a 'repository' and a 'trustee' of the data that the customer has chosen to entrust it with. The legal analogy would be that the customer is the grantor of the asset known as her data, and the digital company that receives and preserves the data is a 'trustee' of that asset. The grantor and the beneficiary of the trust is the customer. The trustee is duty-bound not only to follow the grantor's instructions, but also to act as a fiduciary in the best interests of the beneficiary. The fact that the grantor and the beneficiary are one and the same person in no way changes the obligation of the trustee. This is not just an ethical imperative that sounds nice. It has practical consequences. If digital firms do not embrace the concept of customer data being held in trust, then they run the risk of losing customers and losing the social permission needed to stay in business. This situation is complicated, as customers tend to have strong views on the state having access to their data. Given his distrust of the state, Gandhi would have looked askance at Microsoft's compromises with the Chinese government and would probably have lauded Apple's refusal to hand over customer data 'entrusted' to Apple to the US government (Cook, 2016). In any event, all data-driven firms could help themselves by reading Gandhi and trying to see how they can position themselves away from ownership and in the paradigm of trusteeship. This may end up being both a moral and a practical imperative. Once more the Mahatma turns out to have contemporary relevance.

Gandhi for the State

For the state, the Mahatma advocates creation of an environment where property rights are protected and expropriation is banned, but where an ecosystem is created which encourages voluntary trusteeship on the part of the wealthy. He also makes the practical suggestion of encouraging the wealthy in the interests of their own progeny not to be overly generous in inheritance matters. Oddly enough, Gandhi would have opposed high inheritance taxes and the use of trusts in order to reduce such taxes! A combination of incentives for education and work for the less wealthy, and a frontal attack on 'grinding pauperism', must be the other principles behind the political economy of the Gandhian state. The state has the obligation not to create any hurdles in the path of voluntary action by individuals as they set up trusts. In this context, it is worth considering whether taxes, levies and regulations are a hindrance for the formal organization of trusts. The other question to ask is whether the granting of 'charitable status', with attendant tax-breaks, ends up debilitating the voluntary act and substitutes extrinsic for intrinsic motivation. Another public policy question that needs addressing is whether tax incentives lead to unintended consequences and susceptibility to misuse, which may over time delegitimize the very concept of trusteeship in the eyes of society and become a cause for withdrawal of social permission for all forms of trusts.

Practicality

We revert to the question of the practicality of the Mahatma's seemingly quixotic prescriptions. He addressed this pretty frontally: 'I adhere to my doctrine of trusteeship in spite of the ridicule that has poured upon it. It is true that it is difficult to reach. So is non-violence difficult to attain. But we made up our minds in 1920 to negotiate that steep ascent. We have found it worth the effort' (CW, 1999, v. 81, p. 366). Gandhi was referring to the fact that he had called off a wildly successful civil disobedience movement when violence had entered the movement and several policemen had been killed at a placed called Chauri Chaura. While he was heavily criticized by many of his contemporaries, this one spectacular act set apart the Indian freedom struggle from other political movements in world history. Its final vindication came with the successes of Martin Luther King, Lech Walesa and Nelson Mandela several decades later. If economists and business school professors refuse to engage with the promise and potential of Gandhian ideas, it would be as if political scientists stopped studying the Polish Solidarity movement and the South African Truth and Reconciliation Commission. Ignoring trusteeship is not the appropriate response. Engaging with it, studying it, expanding it, empirically approaching it, re-establishing its connections with the very origins of economics and combining it with contemporary concerns of identity and behavioral nudges— those approaches to trusteeship would be appropriate. And if, in that effort, economics once again becomes a branch of moral philosophy, the benefits may be astonishingly wide-ranging.

Tinkering Gandhi: Perspectives on Human Capital

Gandhi's success in politics was almost entirely dependent on his ability to literally create a dedicated cadre of disciplined and trained followers. It was with this admittedly non-violent 'human capital' that he confronted the economic, military and administrative power of the British Empire, which was, as per the *Hind Swaraj*, inextricably linked up with violence (Parel, HS, 2009). In South Africa, Gandhi was able to get persons from different regions of India who belonged to different classes to volunteer to go to prison. This pattern continued in India, where time and again Gandhi and his followers tested the physical capacities of the British jails. A crucial lesson in discipline to his followers arose when Gandhi dramatically called off his protests after a violent mob incident in Chauri Chaura in the 1920s. As a result, in the later Salt Satyagraha of the 1930s, Gandhi worked out a robustly non-violent movement even in the face of brutal imperial response. Gandhi had succeeded in his education and training of the human capital represented by his followers.

While disciplined non-violence was his principal lesson to his political followers, the charkha and Nai Talim were the Mahatma's contributions in the area of education and training with an eye on the economics of human capital development—and with the implicit goal of attacking 'grinding pauperism' (CW, 1999, v. 15, p. 274). The charkha and Nai Talim rejected several traditions in the learning systems of India, which had been exacerbated by the British education system as introduced into India. Gandhi and his associates J.C. Kumarappa, Hermann Kallenbach, Marjorie Sykes and Maurice Frydman were more in line with the manual labour traditions of Trappist monks, the community traditions of Christian Pietists, the pedagogical methods of Maria Montessori and the empiricist tinkering that was characteristic of James Watt, the Scottish Enlightenment savant. Abandoning Nai Talim and opting for a heavily centralized, examination-oriented, rigid academic system modelled almost exclusively along English boarding school lines has hurt Indian education, and by extension the development of the Indian economy. Gandhi's approach can and perhaps should be grafted on to other approaches (e.g., Atal Tinkering Laboratories) in order to create a more conducive approach for modern economic activity, including the crucial discipline of design. Gandhi in all probability would have almost mischievously seen a connect between Frydman's charkha and Jobs's iPad! In this respect, once again, Gandhi's insights have universal value, going beyond Indian shores.

Afterword

In the years to come, hopefully references to Mahatma Gandhi will exponentially increase in the literature on economics and management and not remain confined to the cloister of 'Gandhian Studies'. In their 2015 paper in the *Journal of Business Ethics*, Balakrishnan, Malhotra and Falkenberg point out that this trend has been slowly catching up. Upadhyaya (1976), Quinn (1996), Pfeffer (1998), Gopinath (2005) and Balasubramanian (2010), along with Balakrishnan et al. in 2017 represent a list that quite candidly is not long enough. When Gandhi goes beyond stakeholder analysis and corporate social responsibility studies and starts cropping up in papers on identity economics, behavioural economics and public policy, we can make the claim that economist Gandhi has arrived. If empirical studies can show that nudges resulting in changes in psychological identity from 'owner' to 'trustee', and from 'manager' to 'trustee', are both possible and have normative consequences, then we will make even more progress. Gandhi's approach to education is surprisingly modern (it embraced twentieth-century Montessori ideas, not nineteenth-century English boarding school ideas) and may hold the key to the more wholesome development of human capital. Gandhi might take his place along with Adam Smith as a profound and seminal thinker who had much to offer in our expanding definitions of homo economicus. Even the thought that the Mahatma referred to Christ as 'the greatest economist of his time' can send a shiver up our spines. Economics might make the connection, not just with a dry agnostic moral philosophy, but with attachment to the sacred, an instinct buried within human beings. Even as we expand our knowledge of the quizzically named Gandhi neurons and the neural dimensions of human trust, we will hopefully keep coming back to the words of this very special, ambivalent and challenging of human beings.

Acknowledgements

It started with Ira Pande of the India International Centre in New Delhi persuading me to write a short piece for her *Quarterly Journal* on the relevance of Gandhi in the context of economic crises and corporate scandals.

I tentatively mentioned this to Prof. Shishir Jha, to whom I owe the kernel of the thought to attempt to expand the study in the context of the broader field of political economy.

At a memorable lunch with Professor Amartya Sen in Cambridge, Massachusetts, I was gently admonished for not having read Smith, the moral philosopher, enough. This was the beginning of an intellectual journey which has been richly rewarding. At an equally memorable dinner a few years later, Prof. Sen's rich elucidation of the difference between wanting to be praiseworthy and seeking praise remains one of the more illuminating lessons I have been privileged to have.

I am indebted to Prof. Siby for pulling my leg for trying to make a subversive attempt to own the Mahatma in capitalist terms and trying to sabotage trusteeship! Nevertheless, he kept telling me that 'there was definitely something worthwhile here'. Prof. Siby's encouragement got me on an exploration that is yet to end. The universal Mahatma has something intelligent, even funny, always sensitive, to say on almost every subject in the world.

Prof. Sirola introduced me to Bilgrami and planted the seed in my mind that Marxist scholars should not have a monopoly on trying to own the Mahatma.

Prof. Rajni Bakshi has undertaken the enormous task of actually tracking down in the *Collected Works* every reference to words like 'trust', 'trustee' and 'trusteeship'. This, of course, is an invaluable resource to any researcher.

Prof. Suhrud managed to find copies of the Trust Deeds of Gandhi's various ashrams. His off-the-cuff insights into the mind of the Mahatma are invariably brilliant gems.

Nothing can substitute the experience of reading and re-reading *Hind Swaraj*. Again, Prof. Siby turned out to be prescient in his insight that *Hind Swaraj* is where Gandhi starts and ends. Naipaul's criticisms, however elegant and clever, miss the context and the range of this classic. Prof. Suhrud successfully dispelled any temptations I might have had to ignore the early Gandhi as 'impractical'. I also strongly recommend to all students repeated reading of the Mahatma's lecture to the economics students at Allahabad University. You suddenly realize how much Gandhi loved and admired the Gospels and how much he knew about them.

Samveg Lalbhai was kind enough to give me a copy of *Anandji Kalyanji Pedhi Nu Itihaas*. I have commissioned a translation. After suitable editing, this might be worth publishing standalone.

Dwijendra Tripathi remains the doyen of Indian business historians. It always pays to read him carefully.

Snell's *Equity* and Maitland's writings on English common law were great reads in and of themselves. MacFarlane's summary is incandescently brilliant. American jurists have also contributed several suitable encomiums to trusteeship as the glory of common law. Tawney's *Religion and the Rise of Capitalism* came highly recommended, but left me a little cold. Loukes's personalized history of the Quakers had the advantage of giving me a sense of how Gandhi might have actually felt about Quakers.

The Isavasya Upanishad was a difficult text to deal with. I found the version by two American scholars (Katz and Egenes) who are influenced by Mahesh Yogi very useful. The version by Swami Krishnananda of the Sivananda Ashram remains a classic.

Smith is repeatedly shortchanged by people who love to quote only one sentence from the *Wealth of Nations*. It might not be a bad idea to include a few chapters of the *Theory of Moral Sentiments* as required readings in every Economics-101 course. Prof. Amartya Sen would certainly approve. It was interesting for me that even as I explored the mind of a twentieth-century self-proclaimed Hindu Bania, I got the opportunity to get solidly acquainted with a giant figure in the Scottish Enlightenment. One could even argue that even without reference to other thinkers, a holistic and balanced re-reading of Smith could very well form the basis of a renewed moral foundation for capitalism. Needless to say, the contemporary work of Akerlof and Kranton builds on this.

Prof. Trupti Mishra kept up a gentle stream of encouragement, arguing that setting economic ideas within a broader historical context will always be worthwhile.

For a 'coming together' of the traditional Indic philosopher Gandhi and the modern political activist Gandhi, there is no one who does a better job than Prof. Anthony Parel. I could argue that without his profound analysis, my own book would not have moved very far. I would be happy if in some small measure I am able to contribute to the coming together of the Indic philosopher Gandhi and the twentieth-century Bania Gandhi.

I am deeply indebted to Prof. Geoffrey Jones who has repeatedly encouraged me to look at the historical context in which ideas emerge. Durban and Bombay were port cities where, in the nineteenth and twentieth centuries, new mercantile activities and new ideas emerged. It is a tribute to Gandhi's genius that he derived inspiration from these settings and used that inspiration to revive and rejuvenate a persistent but weakened national intellectual tradition. Conversations with Prof. Jones on Gandhi, Bajaj, Tandon, Singer, IBM, the Quakers and so much more kept me on my toes.

Prof. Shishir Jha kept me energized through some difficult years, when the dark journeys of the soul seriously threatened to overwhelm me. His intuitive feeling that we had stumbled on something original, something worth saying, helped me stay the course. We stumbled on an added bonus: joint authorship of three standalone papers, one of which has been published.

I subjected my family—my wife Neelambari, my daughter Sanjeevani and my sons Vijayendra and Raghavendra—to torture. I forced them to listen to me droning away chapter by chapter. I am grateful to them for indulging me.

Zainab Daginawalla was invaluable in making up for all my digital inadequacies. The near impossible task of checking out references through the 100-volume *Collected Works* would simply not have happened without her help. She also proved to be an important source of encouragement as she frequently complimented me on the content of the chapters and in addition made some insightful corrections to the text. She is truly a first-rate collaborator.

Prof. Devang Khakhar, director of IITB was very understanding when I went to him and fessed up about some of my personal problems. It is very heartening to see someone so senior in academia being so sensitive.

Prof. Kaushik Basu provided me valuable feedback and removed some of my apprehensions about the book.

Narendra Rajput at IITB-SOM has been my conscience-keeper and guide. His smiling countenance and persistent support have meant much to me.

My indefatigable agent Kanishka Gupta is well-acquainted with the angers, frustrations and occasional ecstasies of a writer's life. He kept company, consoled my soul and gently prodded me on. His friend and colleague Amish Raj Mulmi taught me how to take a piece of research and convert it into a book. I owe him much.

Manish Kumar, my editor at Penguin Random House, approached the text with a gentle scalpel, guided by the instincts of both a lawyer and a historian. It was a pleasure working with him.

Appendix: Note on References

1. In several instances, even for older books, recent editions have been referenced and so indicated.
2. Parel, HS, 2009 stands for the 2009 edition of Gandhi's *Hind Swaraj* edited by Anthony Parel.
3. CW, 1999 stands for the *Collected Works of Mahatma Gandhi*, 1999 edition.
4. The first verse of the Isavasya Upanishad in Roman script is given below:

Isavasyam idam sarvam yat kincha jagatyam jagat
Tena tyaktena bhunjeetha ma gridhah kasya svid dhanam

References

Anandji Kalyanji Pedhi Nu Itihas (n.d.), (Ahmedabad, Private Publication).

Akbar, M.J., *Gandhi's Hinduism: The Struggle Against Jinnah's Islam,* (London, Bloomsbury Publishing India Pvt. Ltd, 2020).

Akerlof, G. and Kranton, R., *Identity Economics,* (Princeton, Princeton UP, 2010).

Arnold, E., *Routledge Revivals: The Song Celestial or Bhagavad-Gita (1906): From the Mahabharata,* (Routledge, 2017).

Bakshi, R., *Bapu Kuti: Journeys in Rediscovery of Gandhi,* (New Delhi, Penguin, 1998).

Bakshi, R., *Bazaars, Conversations and Freedom: For a Market Culture Beyond Greed and Fear,* (New Delhi, Penguin, 2009).

Bakshi, R., *Civilizational Gandhi,* (Mumbai, Gateway House, 2012).

Bakshi, R., *Trusteeship: Business and the Economics of Well-Being,* (Mumbai, Gateway House, 2016).

Balakrishnan, J., Malhotra, A., and Falkenberg, L., 'Multi-Level Corporate Responsibility: A Comparison of Gandhi's Trusteeship with Stakeholder and Stewardship Frameworks', (*Journal of Business Ethics,* 2017), *141*(1), pp. 133–150.

Balasubramanian, N., 'Governing the Socially Responsible Corporation: A Gandhian Perspective', in A. Gupta (ed.), *Ethics, Business and Society: Managing Responsibly,* (New Delhi: SAGE Publications India Pvt. Ltd, 2010), pp. 157–81.

Banerjee, P., Nigam, A., and Pandey, R., 'The Work of Theory. Thinking across Traditions', (*Economic and Political Weekly,* 2016).

Barnett, C., *The Collapse of British Power,* (London, Faber and Faber, 2011).

Becker, G.S., *Human Capital: A Theoretical and Empirical Analysis, with Special Reference to Education,* (Chicago, University of Chicago Press, 1994).

Becker, G.S., *The Economics of Discrimination,* (Chicago, University of Chicago Press, 2010).

Basham, A.L. *The Wonder That Was India,* (New Delhi, India, Picador, 2004).

Bilgrami, A., 'Gandhi and Marx', (*Social Scientist,* 2012), 40 (9/10), pp. 3–25.

Bilgrami, A., *Secularism, Identity, and Enchantment,* (Ranikhet, Permanent Black, 2014).

Bilgrami, A. (ed.) *Marx, Gandhi and Modernity: Essays Presented to Javed Alam,* (Chennai, Tulika Books, 2015).

Bishwanath and Anr vs. Shri Thakur Radhavallabhji and Ors (1967), Supreme Court of India, 1967.

Braudel, F., *Civilization and Capitalism, 15th–18th Century,* S. Reynolds, (trans.), (Berkeley, University of California Press, 1992).

Brown, J.M., *Gandhi: Prisoner of Hope,* (Connecticut, Yale University Press, 1991).

Browning, R., *The Poems of Robert Browning,* (Hertfordshire: Wordsworth Editions Limited, 1994).

Cadbury, A., *Report of the Committee on the Financial Aspects of Corporate Governance,* (London, GEE, 1992).

Caruso, U., 'The Struggle of Right against Might: An Introduction to the Figure of Mahatma Gandhi', in Eva, Pföstl, *Between Ethics and Politics,* (New Delhi, Routledge India, 2016), pp. 20–53.

Chakrabarty, D., *The Calling of History: Sir Jadunath Sarkar and His Empire of Truth,* (Chicago, University of Chicago Press, 2015).

Chaudhuri, N., *The Continent of Circe: Being an Essay on the Peoples of India,* (London, Chatto and Windus, 1965).

Commissioner Of Income Tax vs Jogendra Nath Naskar and Anr, AIR 1965 Cal 570, Calcutta High Court 04 05, 1963.

Constitution of India (1950), (National Portal, Government of India, Ministry of Law and Justice, New Delhi, India, 2018).

Cook, T., 'A Message to Our Customers', (16 February 2016). Source: https://www.apple.com/customer-letter/, retrieved 5 October 2020.

Dadhich, N., 'The Postmodern Discourse on Gandhi: Modernity and Truth', in Allen, Douglas (ed.), *The Philosophy of Mahatma Gandhi for the Twenty-First Century,* (New Delhi, Oxford University Press, 2008), p. 179.

Darwin, C. *The Origin of Species by Means of Natural Selection, or, the Preservation of Favoured Races in the Struggle for Life* (sixth ed., Cambridge library collection), (Cambridge, UK; New York, Cambridge University Press, 2009).

Darwin, C., *The Descent of Man,* (Andesite Press, 2017).

Das, G., *The Difficulty of Being Good: On the Subtle Art of Dharma,* (New Delhi, Oxford University Press, 2010).

Dasgupta, A.K., *Gandhi's Economic Thought,* (London, Routledge, 1996).

Davis, R.H., 'Three Styles in Looting India', *History and Anthropology,* (1994), 6 (4), pp. 293–317.

De Tocqueville, A., *Democracy in America* (vol. 10), (Regency Publishing, 2003).

Desai, R., *Sheth Anandji Kalyanji Pedhi nu Itihas Part 1&2,* (Ahmedabad, Anandji Kalyanji Pedhi, 1983).

Deussen, P., *The Philosophy of the Upanishads,* (New York, Dover Publications, 1966).

Douglas, A., *The Philosophy of Mahatma Gandhi for the Twenty-First Century,* (New Delhi, Oxford University Press, 2008).

Dutt, R.C., *The Economic History of India under Early British Rule: From the Rise of the British Power in 1757 to the Accession of Queen Victoria in 1837,* (Routledge, 2013).

Evans, C., *Quaker Faith and Practice,* fifth edition, (1987).

Fama, E.F., 'Agency Problems and the Theory of the Firm', (*Journal of Political Economy,* 1980), 88 (2), pp. 288–307.

Fischer, L., *The Life of Mahatma Gandhi,* (London, 2015).

Freeman, H., 'Speaking the Language of Quaker Values', (*Friends Journal,* 2016).

Friedman, M., *Essays in Positive Economics,* (Chicago, University of Chicago Press, 1953).

Frydman, M., *Gandhiji, His Life and Work,* (Bombay, Karnatak Publishing House, 1944).

Fukuyama, F., *Trust: The Social Virtues and the Creation of Prosperity,* (Free Press Paperbacks, 1995).

Gandhi R., *Why Gandhi Still Matters: An Appraisal of the Mahatma's Legacy,* (New Delhi, Aleph, 2017).

Gandhi, I., *Selected Speeches of Indira Gandhi: August 1969–August 1972,* (Publications Division, Ministry of Information and Broadcasting, Government of India, 1975).

Gandhi, M.K. and Fischer, L., (ed.), *The Essential Gandhi. An Anthology of His Writings on His Life, Work and Ideas,* (New York, Vintage Books, 2002).

Gandhi, M.K., *The Collected Works of Mahatma Gandhi*, (New Delhi, Publications Division Government of India, 1999), referenced as CW, 1999.

Gandhi, M.K., *My Picture of Free India*, A.T. Hingorani (ed.), (Bombay, Bharatiya Vidya Bhavan, 1965). Source: https://www.gandhiheritageportal.org/ghp_booksection_detail/Ny02OTMtMg==#page/8/mode/2up

Gandhi, M.K. and Parel, A., (ed.), *Hind Swaraj and Other Writings,* centenary edition, (New Delhi: Cambridge University Press, 2009), referenced as Parel, HS, 2009. Gandhi, M.K., *Constructive Programme: Its Meaning and Place,* (New Delhi, Prabhat Prakashan, 2015).

Gandhi, R., *The Good Boatman: A Portrait of Gandhi*, (New Delhi, Penguin Books, 2018).

Gandhi, M.K., *An Autobiography: Or the Story of My Experiments with Truth*, (London, Penguin, 2001).

Gopinath, C., 'Trusteeship as a Moral Foundation for Business', *(Business and Society Review,* 2005), 110 (3), pp. 331–344.

Goswami, C., *Globalisation Before Its Time. The Gujarati Merchants from Kachchh,* (New Delhi, Penguin, 2016).

Graves, R., *The Greek Myths: The Complete and Definitive Edition,* (London, Penguin, 2011).

Graves, R., *Good-bye to All That: An Autobiography,* (London, Penguin Books, 2014).

Gregory, P., *Gandhi's Interpreter: A Life of Horace Alexander,* (Edinburgh University Press, 2010).

Griffith, R., *The Texts of the White Yajurveda,* (New Delhi, India, Munshiram Manoharlal Publishers, 1987).

Guha, R., 'The Last Quaker in India', *(The Hindu).* Source: http://www.thehindu.com/todays-paper/tp-features/tp-sundaymagazine/the-last-quaker-in-india/article2275127.ece

Guha, R., *Gandhi before India,* (New Delhi, Penguin, 2013).

Guha, R., *Gandhi: The Years That Changed the World 1914–1948*, (Gurgaon, Penguin, 2018).

Gulley, P., *Living the Quaker Way: Discover the Hidden Happiness in the Simple Life,* (London, Convergent, 2013).

Hayek, F.A., *The Road to Serfdom: Text and Documents: The Definitive Edition*, (Routledge, 2014).

Hume, D., *Essays: Moral, Political, and Literary,* vol. 1. (HardPress Publishing, 2012).

Hutchesson, *The All England Law Reports*, 1991.

Introduction/Seth Anandji Kalyanji Firm, (n.d.), *Anandji Kalyanji Pedhi*. Source: http://www.anandjikalyanjipedhi.org/aboutus.php, retrieved 1 March 2017.

Jahanbegloo, R., *The Gandhian Moment*, (Massachusetts, Harvard University Press, 2013).

Jahanbegloo, R., *Letters to a Young Philosopher*, (New Delhi, Oxford University Press, 2018).

Jensen, M.C., and Meckling, W.H., 'Theory of the Firm: Managerial Behavior, Agency Costs and Ownership Structure', (*Journal of Financial Economics*, 1976), 3 (4), pp. 305–360.

John, P., 'Bapu had implored the wealthy to emulate Chinubhai: Ahmedabad News', (*Times of India*, 1 February, 2018). Source: https://timesofindia.indiatimes.com/city/ahmedabad/bapu-had-implored-the-wealthy-to-emulate-chinubhai/articleshow/62734432.cms, Retrieved 10 October 2020.

Jones, G., Kothandaraman, P.K., and Herman, K., 'Jamnalal Bajaj, Mahatma Gandhi and the Struggle for Indian Independence', (Harvard Business School Case 807028-2006, 2006).

Jones, G., and Kiron, D., 'Globalizing Consumer Durables: Singer Sewing Machine Before 1914', (Harvard Business School Case 804-001, 2017).

Kamali, M.H., *Principles of Islamic Jurisprudence*, (The Islamic Texts Society, 2002).

Kane, P.V., *History of Dharmasastra*, (Poona, Bhandarkar Oriental Research Institute, 1958).

Katz, V., and Egenes, T., *The Upanishads. A New Translation*, (New York, Penguin Random House, 2015).

Kierkegaard, S., *Provocations: Spiritual Writings of Kierkgaard*, (New York, Plough Publishing House, 2014).

Kolge, N., *Gandhi against Caste*, (New Delhi, Oxford University Press, 2017).

Krishnananda, S., (n.d.), *Commentary on the Isavasya Upanishads*, (Rishikesh, The Divine Life Society, 2017).

Krishnananda, S. (n.d.), *Essays on the Upanishads*, (Rishikesh, The Divine Life Society, 2017).

Krishnananda, S. (n.d.), *Isavasya Upanishad for Beginners,* (Rishikesh, The Divine Life Society, 2017).

Kumarappa, J.C., *Gandhian Economic Thought,* (AB Sarva Seva Sangh Prakashan, 1951).

Kumarappa, J.C., *Economy of Permanence: A Quest for a Social Order Based on Non-Violence,* (Varanasi, Sarva Seva Sangh Prakashan, 2010).

Lewis, W.A., 'Economic Development with Unlimited Supplies of Labour', (*The Manchester School of Economic and Social Studies*, 1954), vol. 22, no. 2, pp. 139–191.

Lira, C., *Biography of James Watt*, (2001). Source: https://www.egr.msu.edu/~lira/supp/steam/wattbio.html

Loukes, H., *The Discovery of Quakerism,* (1960).

M Siddiq (D) Thr Lrs v. Mahant Suresh Das & Ors, Supreme Court of India, 9 November 2019.

MacCulloch, D., *A History of Christianity: The First Three Thousand Years,* (London, Penguin, 2010).

Macfarlane, A., *The Making of the Modern World: Visions from the West and East*, (Hampshire, Palgrave, 2002).

Maine, H., *Village-Communities in the East and West,* (Miami, HardPress, 2018).

Maitland, F.W., *Equity: A Course of Lectures,* (Cambridge University Press, 2011).

Marx, K., and Engels, F., *The Communist Manifesto,* (London, Penguin, 2002).

Matthews, R., *Jinnah vs. Gandhi*, (London, Hachette UK, 2012).

McGhee, J., *Snell's Equity,* (London, Sweet & Maxwell, 2017).

MHRD (2020), New Education Policy 2020. Source: https://www.mhrd.gov.in/sites/upload_files/mhrd/files/NEP_Final_English_0.pdf, retrieved 5 October 2020.

Mincer, J., 'Investment in Human Capital and Personal Income Distribution', (*The Journal of Political Economy*, 1958), vol. 66, pp. 281–302.

Mondhe, A., 'Nelson Mandela: The "South African Gandhi"'. Source: DW: http://www.dw.com/en/nelson-mandela-the-south-african-gandhi/a-6631520, retrieved 6 October 2011.

Mukherjee, M., 'Justice, War, and the Imperium: India and Britain in Edmund Burke's Prosecutorial Speeches in the Impeachment Trial of Warren Hastings', (*Law and History Review*, 2005), 23 (3), pp. 589–630.

Mukherjee, S., 'Matter or Spirit'. Source: https://swarajyamag.com/magazine/matter-or-spirit, (2015).

Naipaul, V.S., *India: A Million Mutinies Now,* (London, Minerva, 1990).

Naipaul, V.S., *India: A Wounded Civilization,* (London, Picador, 2012).

Nandy, A., *The Intimate Enemy,* (New Delhi, Oxford University Press, 2009).

Nandy, A., *Regimes of Narcissism, Regimes of Despair,* (New Delhi, Oxford University Press, 2013).

Naoroji, D., *Poverty and Un-British Rule in India,* (Nabu Press, 2010).

Narayan, R.K., *Waiting for the Mahatma,* (New Delhi, Penguin, 2010).

NITI Ayog (2019). Atal Tinkering Labs. Source: https://niti.gov.in/, retrieved 5 October 2020.

North, D., *Institutions, Institutional Change and Economic Performance,* (Cambridge University Press, 1990).

O'Brien, C.C., *The Great Melody: A Thematic Biography of Edmund Burke,* (London, Faber Finds, 2015).

Orwell, G., *Essays,* (London, Penguin, 2000).

Parel, A., *Gandhi's Philosophy and the Quest for Harmony,* (New Delhi, Cambridge University Press, 2006).

Parel, A.J., *Pax Gandhiana: The Political Philosophy of Mahatma Gandhi,* (New Delhi, Oxford University Press, 2016).

Pfeffer, J., *The Human Equation: Building Profits by Putting People First,* (Boston, Harvard Business School Press, 1998).

Phillipson, N., *Adam Smith: An Enlightened Life,* (London, Penguin UK, 2010).

Pigou, A., *A Study in Public Finance,* (London, Macmillan, 1928).

Pisupati, B., 'Environment, Biodiversity and Gandhiji', (*The Hindu,* 2 October 2011). Source: http://www.thehindu.com/news/national/environment-biodiversity-and-gandhiji/article2504124.ece.

Prabhu, J., 'Gandhi's Religious Ethics', in Allen, Douglas (ed.), *The Philosophy of Mahatma Gandhi for the Twenty-First Century,* (New Delhi, Oxford University Press, 2008), p. 163.

Pramatha Nath Mullick vs Pradyumna Kumar Mullick, 27 BOMLR 1064, Bombay High Court, 28 April 1925.

Quinn, R.E., *Deep Change,* (San Francisco, Jossey-Bass, 1996).

Radhakrishnan, S., *The Principal Upanisads,* (Noida, HarperCollins, 2006).

Radhakrishnan, S., *Mahatma Gandhi: Essays and Reflections on His Life and Thought,* (Mumbai, Jaico, 2010).

Radhakrishnan, S., *The Bhagavadgita,* (Blackie & Son, 1979).

Rajan, R., *The Third Pillar: How Markets and the State Leave the Community Behind,* (New Delhi, Harper Collins, 2019).

Ram Jankijee Deities & Ors vs State of Bihar and Ors, (1999) 5 SCC 50, Supreme Court of India, 11 May 1999.

Ramachandran, V.S., *The Tell-Tale Brain,* (Random House, India, 2011).

Rao, J., 'Beyond Racism: The Story of Prakash Tandon and Unilever India', (*Harvard Business History Review,* Spring 2014).

Rathore, A.S. and Mohapatra, R., *Hegel's India: A Reinterpretation, with Texts,* (New Delhi, Oxford University Press, 2017).

Redkar, C., *Gandhian Engagement with Capital: Perspective of J.C. Kumarappa,* (New Delhi, SAGE Publications, 2019).

Rengarajan, L.S., 'A Gandhian Life', (*The Hindu,* 24 July 2005). Source: https://www.thehindu.com/thehindu/mag/2005/07/24/stories/2005072400130400.htm

Reynolds, R., *The White Sahibs in India,* (M. Secker & Warburg, Limited, 1937 [archived in 2016]).

Rothermund, D., *Mahatma Gandhi: An Essay in Political Biography,* vol. 5, (Manohar Publishers, 1992).

Rowntree, B.S., *Poverty: A Study of Town Life,* (Macmillan, 2009).

Rudolph, L.I. and Rudolph, S.H., *The Modernity of Tradition: Political Development in India.* (Chicago, University of Chicago Press, 1984).

Rudolph, L.I. and Rudolph, S.H., *Postmodern Gandhi and Other Essays: Gandhi in the World and at Home,* (Chicago, University of Chicago Press, 2010).

Ruskin, J. and Holt, R.V., (ed.), *Unto This Last,* (Chelsea House, 1983).

Satyamurty, G., 'A Non-Conformist Genius Architects of Coimbatore', (*The Hindu,* 10 January 2009). Source: https://www.thehindu.com/todays-paper/tp-national/tp-tamilnadu/A-non-conformist-genius-Architects-Of-Coimbatore/article16348764.ece, retrieved 5 October 2020.

Schultz, T., 'Investment in Human Capital', (*American Economic Review*, 1961), vol. 51, No 1, pp. 1–17.

Scott, A.W., 'The Trust as an Instrument of Law Reform', (*Yale Law Journal,* 1922), 31.5 , pp. 457–68.

Scott, J.B., *Spiritual Despots: Modern Hinduism and the Genealogies of Self-Rule,* (Chicago, University of Chicago Press, 2016).

Scruton, R., *The Soul of the World,* (New Jersey, Princeton University Press, 2014).

Sen, A., *The Argumentative Indian: Writings on Indian History, Culture, and Identity,* (Harmondsworth, Allen Lane, 2005).

Sen, A., *Identity and Violence: The Illusion of Destiny,* (New Delhi, Penguin Books India, 2007).

Sen, A., 'Adam Smith and the Contemporary World', (*Erasmus Journal for Philosophy and Economics,* 2010), 3 (1), pp. 50–67.

Shankara, A., *The Isa, Kena and Mundaka Upanishads and Sri Sankara's Commentary,* (G.A. Natesan & Co., 1905).

Sharma, B.N.K., *History of the Dvaita School of Vedanta and its Literature*, vol. 1, (Motilal Banarsidass Publisher, 1960).

Sheean, V., *Mahatma Gandhi: A Great Life in Brief,* (New Delhi, Ministry of Information & Broadcasting, Government of India, New Delhi, 2005).

Sheean, V., *Mahatma Gandhi: A Great Life in Brief,* (Publications Division, Ministry of Information & Broadcasting, 2018).

Shirer, W., *Gandhi: A Memoir,* (New York, Simon and Schuster, 1980).

Smith, A., *The Wealth of Nations,* (New Delhi, Penguin Books, 1982).

Smith, A., *The Theory of Moral Sentiments,* (Cambridge University Press, 2002).

Subramanian, A., *The Caste on Merit,* (New Delhi, Harper Collins, 2020).

Sundaram, P.S., *Tiruvalluvar: The Kural,* (New Delhi, Penguin Books, 1990).

Sunstein, C., and Thaler, R., *Nudge* (New Haven, 2008).

Sykes, M., *The Story of Nai Talim: Fifty Years of Education at Sevagram, India, 1937-1987* (first ed.), (New Delhi, National Council of Educational Research and Training, 2009).

Thaler, R.H., and Ganser, L.J., *Misbehaving: The Making of Behavioral Economics,* (New York, WW Norton, 2015).

Thaler, R.H., and Sunstein, C.R., *Nudge: Improving Decisions About Health, Wealth, and Happiness,* (London, Penguin Books, 2010).

Tirole, J., *Economics for the Common Good,* (New Jersey, Princeton University Press, 2017).

Tripathi, D. and Mehta, M.J., *The Nagarsheth of Ahmedabad: The History of an Urban Institution in a Gujarat City*, in *Proceedings of the Indian History Congress*, (1978), vol. 39, pp. 481–496.

Upadhyaya, R.B., *Social Responsibility of Business and the Trusteeship Theory of Mahatma Gandhi,* (New Delhi, Sterling Publishers, 1976).

Veblen, T., *The Theory of the Leisure Class,* (Routledge, 2017).

Vivekananda, S., and Nikhilananda, S., *Vivekananda: The Yogas and Other Works*, (Ramakrishna-Vivekananda Centre, 1953).

Weber, M., *The Protestant Ethic and the Spirit of Capitalism, and Other Writings,* (New York, Routledge, 2006).